I CHOOSE MENOPAUSE!

I CHOOSE MENOPAUSE!

Love Your Hormones & HRT...
A Practical & Positive Tale

JANE PANGBOURNE

authors
AND CO.

First published in Great Britain in 2024
by Authors & Co.
www.authorsandco.pub

Copyright © Jane Pangbourne 2024

Jane Pangbourne asserts the moral right to be identified as the
author of this work in accordance with the Copyright, Designs and
Patents Act 1988.

ISBN 978-1-915771-86-5 (paperback)
ISBN 978-1-915771-87-2 (hardback)

CONTENTS

ABOUT THE AUTHOR

Jane Pangbourne is based in the UK and is married to Roger. Between them, they have four grown-up children.

Jane has studied menopause and female health for many years, and as a qualified nutritionist and certificated women's health practitioner, she loves anything gut or medically oriented; regularly developing and sharing easy to digest resources and information about female health and hormones.

Many years ago, Jane realised that her creative brain would not be controlled by managers or company rules, so she was always going to make a difference in her own unique way. She views regrets as a waste of energy and firmly believes that failure helps to shape us, but possibly wishes she had studied to be a doctor. Given her passion for medicine, she feels she may have wasted an opportunity, but she has since strived hard to make up for earlier decisions.

You are invited to learn how and why Jane came to help confused, exhausted and often angry women to become less confused, exhausted and angry, and how she has successfully steered many thousands from feeling lost and belittled regarding their health; to taking back control and getting on with their lives.

Please throw yourself into this book with an open mind, a light heart and a desire to get the most from your menopausal years.

You will discover that nothing you may currently be experiencing is new, shocking or embarrassing. It's more common than you would believe.

Welcome to this book and to your new normal.

GET IN TOUCH:

My website:
https://www.menopausalnotmad.co.uk

My Instagram:
https://www.instagram.com/menopausalnotmad/

My Facebook page:
https://www.facebook.com/menopausalnotmad/

Email:
jane@menopausalnotmad.co.uk

ACKNOWLEDGMENTS

Thank you to everyone who has contributed to my own positive self-perception over the years; particularly to my ever-patient husband Roger, who has built me up to expect more of myself and who supports me in everything I do, even when I'm being a dick! I could not have achieved what I have without him.

To our children, who had years of dealing with an erratic, perimenopausal version of me. I hope the subsequent HRT-supplemented years have been easier.

To my mum, who passed away in 2011. She did her utmost to help me become my best self, whilst allowing me the freedom to fail along the way. I now know how her life became so much more challenging after having her HRT taken away following media scaremongering. I have tried to stop the same from happening to others. I hope she would be proud of who I have become.

To my stepdad, who passed away in recent years. Quiet and reflective, he made my mum very happy and was a fabulous grandad to my children. He never forgot that I commandeered his leather jacket when I was sixteen, but I think he forgave me!

To my sweet-natured big brother, Mark. We were rubbish at staying in touch but since losing our parents, we have made a concerted effort to do just that. My life is richer for having him and his family as part of it. He no longer tries to bribe me to leave him alone as he did in the 1980s.

I want to thank my few true friends, both longer-term and more recent, who have supported me and allowed me to just do my thing whilst being there when I needed to vent, chat or just giggle. I hope you know who you are and that you are very precious to me.

Special thanks to Rachel who has stood by me since we were twelve years old. She has always been there in the wings with no judgment and no agenda, ready to scoop me up when I made poor choices, and there were plenty of poor choices! I value that loyalty and support more than she knows and am proud to have been called her friend for over forty-five years.

A short note to the anonymous and the known people who have aimed online abuse at me or chosen to behave very unpleasantly towards me for reasons best known to them. I am not ashamed to say that I have felt hurt by every single unkind word and deed, but my coping mechanisms are strong, and I have learnt more about life every time it has happened. I no longer allow space for such negativity in my head or my life, which has fostered more creativity and growth, so for that I'm thankful.

INTRODUCTION

HOPE

This book is like you and me. It's not just one thing. It doesn't tick just one box or sing in just one key. I aim to impart both facts and my lived experiences in the same way I do with all my support and guidance of women. It is composed of blended facts, thoughts, experiences and years of ongoing study.

I happily share health and hormone information in my no-nonsense style, whilst taking you on a little walk through some of my own life. My aim is for you to accept and enjoy menopause in the most practical and positive way possible.

I will talk primarily about menopause and hormone replacement therapy (HRT) but also about my personal experiences with hormones, hysterectomy and making the best of things at every opportunity, to provide context and to inform in a light-hearted manner. I hope my informal style will help you feel less of an outsider as you deal with your erratic moods, hot flushes, dry vagina and any other menopausal symptoms you may be experiencing.

I could have written a whole book about hormone replacement alone, but instead I have selected the key areas women often ask me about and usually misunderstand, as we were never taught about our own bodies.

I have presented these topics through my own lens as an everyday human with a head full of knowledge and a desire to simplify stuff to help you thrive.

Nothing in here should be considered medical advice. It is all based on my lived experiences, professional practice and educational studies.

PERCEPTION

I totally understand that your perception of menopause and HRT may be a little different from the reality and that's ok. It's a minefield of fake facts out there.

Even in the bleakest of times, I can find the positive in anything, which can be quite annoying I suppose, but I try to pepper that with a strong dose of ranting too. It's all about balance.

What this book is NOT

Although the following pages outline and clarify facts, and although you will also learn a lot about menopause, HRT and mindset by reading them; they do not form a menopause manual.

Nor will you learn how to meditate or use crystals and magnets to heal yourself. I leave that to others as it's just not my bag. That's not to say I don't love an essential oil or a nice massage, but neither will solve the longer-term challenges of depleting hormone levels.

Think of these pages as a chat with me over a cuppa; about life, love and experience, with a big dose of hormones, menopause and HRT thrown in.

I've popped the kettle on ready for us to get started.

DISRUPTIVE

I am considered to be quite disruptive. My experiences have played a part in that, just as your experiences play a big part in *your* approach to life; but regardless of your past, you're in charge now.

I urge you to start feeling comfortable talking about your body and how it works. Share your menopausal symptoms and HRT experiences with friends and family, but don't compare them with your own. You are unique and your menopause will be unique too.

Share but don't compare. I do love a rhyme.

I have worked hard to ensure that my words are not only correct at the time of writing, but also relatable and expressed in my usual easy to digest format. Whether it's a video, a social media post, a face-to-face meeting or this book, I always try to answer your questions and concerns in the way I would have wanted someone to talk to me in my late thirties, when I was perimenopausal. .. Yes, you can be perimenopausal in your thirties, but more on that later.

I include my own experiences of menopause and HRT, along with guidance for you to take into your life to help you get on with, well you know… getting on.

Hot flushes are just one of the challenges of menopause but seemingly the most often talked about. I do remember experiencing them a long time ago in my pre-HRT days, but we are complex beings and menopause is definitely more than the odd flush or forgetting why you went upstairs.

When it comes to simplifying the wide range of symptoms, including feelings of low mood, irritability, dry skin, low sex drive, hair loss or any of the other symptoms you may be experiencing, I find that having somebody hear and acknowledge your worries is often as impactful as the solutions and guidance offered, although I do love a solution.

I hope you find my words mostly helpful, sometimes inspiring, and occasionally humorous and I hope you also feel supported in your menopause experience along the way.

I hope you will stay within my world after reading my words, but mostly, I hope you feel able to embrace all the good things that await you in your post-menopausal years, without fear or judgment from anyone else, whilst bungee jumping into your new normal - Bungee jumping not compulsory.

Much love,

Jane x

HORMONES AND MENOPAUSE

A Brief Truth

Female hormones can be annoying little shits. There! I've said it and I'm not taking it back.

To cut the hormones some slack, they do have some great attributes like creating a sex drive, making pregnancy possible, and generally keeping us healthy.

It's not always their fault when they misbehave. We often don't look after them consistently with our lifestyle choices but there is no judgment from me on that score. I can inhale a family-sized bag of crisps in one sitting with the best of them and I do love a glass of wine. Sometimes it's a matter of not giving yourself a hard time when you don't do everything right.

Life can be cruel, challenging and honestly quite ridiculous at times, so, if you feel unworthy, lost or guilty, I want to help you to become better informed and feel more in control. **The alternative to menopause isn't hugely appealing.**

My overall aim is to shine a light on the many and varying elements which form our fragile self-perception, and our understanding of hormones and of the world. After many years working within the world of menopause, I know you can make friends with your hormones and in fact grow to love them a little bit, even when it may seem as if they hate you.

HRT Untruths

I expect you've heard or read things about menopause and HRT that are not true. Here are three of my least favourite.

"If you're still having periods, you can't be perimenopausal."

This totally grinds my gears. The whole concept of *peri*menopause is that this is the time *before* menopause. Menopause is when your periods stop completely.

If you're still having periods but have menopausal symptoms this is a clear indication of *peri*menopause.

"You can only take HRT for (insert random number) years."

Our hormones are very important for our health and almost every cell in the female body has an estrogen receptor attached to it. We are all individuals with individual needs, desires and health histories, so, there is no pre-set HRT time-frame which is appropriate for everyone and I for one will never be stopping my HRT.

"Testosterone is a male hormone, and women will be at risk of harm if they take it."

Oh please. Stop it.

This is so commonly stated that I am considering having a tattoo on my forehead saying, *Women need testosterone too!*

It's true that men produce more testosterone than women, but women really do need testosterone. In fact, before perimeno-pause women produce three to four times more testosterone than estrogen, at a level of around one-tenth that of a man. It is an important hormone for sex drive, muscle strength, mood and much more.

Incidentally, men also produce the 'female' hormone estrogen. Who knew?

You will not grow a penis or a beard if you supplement with the lower female dose of testosterone when you need it. I for one am grateful to be able to replenish my testosterone every day.

Chapter One
─────────────

AND SO, IT BEGINS

YOUNG AND FEISTY

I am all about taking control of our own future and I'm not a believer in fate, but we don't really have the luxury of that control when we're young as we are, in the main, managed by our parents or carers.

My dad worked around the UK and aboard when I was growing up which, in addition to regular house moves in the UK, resulted in the whole family being moved abroad. It sounds exciting and I suppose it was at times, but my over-arching memory is one of not being settled and never having put down roots.

I am very much a product of this upbringing. My memories of going to kindergarten in Argentina (known as pre-school or nursery in the UK), where I lived from the ages of about two to five, may seem totally irrelevant, but these experiences formed the beginnings of what made me the practical meno-pause educator of today.

I was a bubbly young girl, but also I now believe, on the neurodivergent spectrum. I had and still have, a very busy mind, an inability to focus, sometimes hyper-focus, and a tendency to procrastinate as if my life depended on it.

I know more about such things now and view my quirks as my superpower. I embrace my creativity and passions with no self-judgment. It is very liberating and has given me a fabulous insight into the challenges experienced by my neurodivergent menopause community members.

> *Side Note*
>
> Estrogen is key to balance in the body, and this includes the brain. Women are excellent at masking neurodivergent traits, but perimenopause makes that so much more difficult. Racing thoughts, anxiety and reduced confidence may well be caused by low or fluctuating estrogen accentuating your expertly masked neurodivergence.

You may have been told you were 'too much', 'flaky' or 'spiky' as you grew up. If so, then I hear you, my friend. It's worthwhile taking a moment to consider your own superpower(s).

Even when I was as young as two or three, I remember feeling that people just didn't 'get me'. I recall feeling confused and angry when the kindergarten children and teachers couldn't understand my creative ways and, let's be honest, quite opinionated attitude.

My mum was called into the kindergarten office more than once to discuss my progress. As a primary, and later, special educational needs teacher, you can imagine her delight at that.

I was feisty, and my teachers felt I was unsociable. I was *not* unsociable, but when I reflect on those days I feel empathy for that girl who was only trying to work out how to be.

I used to think those early days totally defined the adult version of me, but they really didn't. It took me many years to realise that I am in control and am no longer that little child trying to fit in.

You're in control of you too, you know. Who wants to fit in anyway? Who are we trying to fit in with? I'm bloody brilliant at being me and you are the absolute best at being you so there should be no issues there, but I know it can be challenging.

This might be a good opportunity for you to consider your own self-perception at a young age, and the path that brought you to where you are now. If you're finding menopause a challenge, it does make it easier to try to come to terms with your past.

PERIODS

We often have a rose-tinted memory of how great we felt before perimenopause. We forget that our hormones seem to have been trying to piss us off for most of our lives.

On Christmas Eve, aged thirteen, I was thrilled to realise that I had started my periods, and I was now a grown-up. I was a relatively late bloomer from a physical perspective, but seemingly overnight developed a shelf of boobs which took all my efforts to cover up. Body positivity wasn't a thing in the 1980s.

I don't think I even knew there was a thing called menopause at that age. I expect like many of you, I come from an era when boobs, periods, lady parts… no, that's not what I call them now!… and later, menopause, were most definitely off the table for open conversation.

I will take this opportunity to give huge credit to my mum who, from the time I was around seven years old, talked to me about the basics of how babies are made and what periods are all about. I think she would enjoy my openness about such things now. However, even then, I still couldn't go into a shop to buy my own sanitary towels or tampons for many years. The shame was just too much.

My hormonal teen brain had such mixed-up messages going on. So proud to be growing up but so ashamed to acknowledge how that manifests in the body. The teenage brain is still growing and learning but we are fooled into thinking we need to know what we want, have it all planned out and that we should have our shit together by the time we leave school. Even making curriculum choices at thirteen or fourteen seems a lot to expect.

When I was growing up, I felt immense pressure to behave in a mature manner with no real acknowledgment of the fact that at thirteen most of us don't have a bloody clue what we're doing and we're just riding the hormone wave whilst trying to see where we fit in with the world.

I have built a global brand around being the person who doesn't fit in. Other people's opinions of me are really none of my business. I want you to feel the same about your life and future and to have the encouragement and tools to dance flamboyantly into your peri and post-menopausal years with confidence, and a desire *not* to fit in.

I'm terrible at revising for exams or adapting to new technical processes, but my brain retains a lot of seemingly useless information, and my visual memory is a plucky little beast, so I've always found a way to do what's needed to achieve my goals, either at school, college, university or work.

Maybe, since those hormones started their fun little game of fluctuations, you've been mourning the loss of your own previously excellent memory or that confidence you took for granted as a ballsy young woman.

You may have developed a new fear of driving, which is a common problem for peri and post-menopausal women as the estrogen decline affects the part of the brain that feeds our confidence. In my early perimenopausal years. I was an adult tutor and verifier, working all over the country and I clearly remember having to stop the car on numerous occasions as the anxiety would be overwhelming. Incidentally, I had no idea what anxiety was at that time, so possibly like you, I felt completely unprepared.

I was definitely negatively affected by my hormones as I grew up, but in the seventies and eighties we kind of accepted that period flooding, very low mood and pain were all just part of life, and this was the way things were. With no internet and little information about hormones at that age, *we just got on with it.* We now know better but there is still a long way to go in the study and treatment of female health.

> **Side Note**
>
> I have developed a huge dislike of the phrase 'just got on with it'. It epitomises the attitude – still way too prevalent in the year 2024 – that women should 'get on with menopause' or that we will 'get through it'.
>
> Menopause is all the time after your periods have stopped, which may be more than half your life, depending on your personal health history, so 'getting through' menopause would mean the end of life.

My friend, Rachel, whom I have known since I was twelve years old, and refer to in my acknowledgments, struggled badly with her hormones, which turned out to be an undiagnosed condition known as adenomyosis.

Rachel outlines her experience better than I ever could:

"As a teenager, I was plagued with painful and heavy periods. I would experience flooding on the first couple of days of my period which was hugely embarrassing during my teen years. I remember feeling self-conscious in case of any leaks onto my school skirt and this happened from time to time.

I had very painful stomach cramps which would make me feel faint and washed out and I regularly took painkillers for the first couple of days of my period. I was prescribed various contraceptive pills to keep my symptoms under control, but none really worked. I was told I had endometriosis but was never offered any other type of treatment.

Over the years I learned to live with the condition, as a young woman right through to perimenopause. It was only when I entered menopause, after taking HRT for a time and having scans for problem bleeding, that I was offered further treatment which in my case was a Mirena coil.

This did not cure the issue and after a few complications during various procedures, I was subsequently diagnosed with adeno-myosis and have since had a hysterectomy at the age of fifty-six."

— **Rachel Swain, May 2024**

I am so happy Rachel has now had a hysterectomy, which was absolutely the right decision for her. Now she can get on with enjoying her post-hysterectomy life.

Unlike me, she didn't feel the need to ask her surgeon for a photo of her removed uterus, cervix, fallopian tubes and ovaries as I had done when I had my own hysterectomy. To be fair, most don't and it's not compulsory, but you know I love anything medical.

More on my hysterectomy story in Chapter Seven.

At this point, you may like to consider your expectations of your own hormones. It's always good to have a realistic plan to keep them accountable. What do you want from them? What's not working for you?

DON'T TALK TO ME

In 1982 I was fifteen years old and obviously knew everything about life. In my opinion at the time, my parents had no clue about the world or how I felt, so I preferred not to speak to them unless I had to.

It was usually just my mum or older brother at home with me, whilst my dad worked away, which suited me as I didn't want much parental intervention. My parents had always reassured me that they would never split up, so from a stability perspective, all seemed fine.

I am aware that I appear like a psychologist's dream with all my parental, attachment and abandonment worries, but I promise you, I have worked hard to understand myself over the years and I am very self-aware so it's all good. (If I was allowed to insert a smiley face emoji here, I would, but it would greatly upset my editor)

Having moved house numerous times, I was determined to squeeze every ounce of enjoyment out of my friendships for fear of moving house yet again. On each occasion, I was wrenched away from my friends and from the life I had built for myself.

My dad had promised that we wouldn't move for at least ten years following our move when I was around nine years old but, as I had half suspected would happen, after three years, we were off again. That move had hurt the most as I had taken some time to adjust, was doing well at school and had grown to love my life there.

I merely mention this as further insight into what made me the resilient person I am today.

Being the new girl at school every two or three years had become more than a little tedious and this time I had no plans to toe the line. I tried to ignore the nagging internal urges to fit in, comply and gain approval from everyone. A rebel by nature but a people pleaser in the making.

There followed years of smoking behind the bike sheds and underage drinking at parties whenever the opportunity arose.

At aged fifteen, we had lived in our house for three years so there was a high risk of moving again, and by now I knew a lot about making new friends. I'd become an expert at that but knew little about maintaining effective relationships. What was the point when I was never allowed to stay?

As soon as I could, I found myself a part-time job as a Saturday girl in a hairdresser about 40 minutes away on the bus. I earned £3.50 for a nine-hour day, which was a really poor wage even in those days. I hated it, but I needed to be busy, and craved some independence. The staff members were quite mean, but, feisty as I was, I allowed this until I was able to find an alternative role which became a pattern of my working life until I discovered my own skills and self-worth.

The fact I still remember how the staff members made me feel, is an indication of the impact it had on my self-esteem, but it taught me a lot about people and how *not* to behave which I view to be a great life lesson. Every cloud and all that.

DEAR DIARY

One day I was hacking away at the thick pages of the book I had selected for mutilation, leaving red dents in my thumb and forefinger from the hard plastic handles of the scissors.

I had no intention of allowing my mum to read my inner feelings. Even though I had no reason to suspect my mum would try to read my diary, I was taking no chances, so had decided to cut a diary-sized chunk out of the inside of one of my old storybooks to secretly house the thoughts and anguishes of my fifteen-year-old mind.

I began to use my diary as my confidante and totally trustworthy friend. My diary knew all my intimate feelings and never judged or commented on my rantings.

"Dear Diary… I am worried that I may be pregnant! Not because I have done anything, because I haven't, but I've been told that there are other ways to become pregnant like pools and toilets, etc."

This sentence, taken directly from my first diary, is both sad and hilarious to me.

Sad, as it clearly demonstrates how fake information can spread, and hilarious as I am now a female wellness and HRT educator. Fortunately, I do now know the finer details of how we get pregnant! However, even in this modern age, many women do not know key information about their own bodies, and this breaks my menopausal heart.

I remember being taught about sanitary towels and tampons at age thirteen. No boys were permitted to attend the class, which is ridiculous of course, and by that time most of the girls had started their periods anyway so it was kind of redundant information by then.

Research led by Professor Joyce Harper at University of London, University College (UCL) EGS Institute for Women's Health in 2023, showed that over ninety percent of women had never been educated about menopause at school but that over sixty percent started to look for information when they experienced menopausal symptoms.

Things are improving very slowly in the UK, and menopause has been covered in secondary schools since September 2020 as part of the relationships, health and sex curriculum, but we have so much more to do to help people understand that our hormones shouldn't be demonised. The craving for fact-based information on menopause is understandably boundless in my online and real-life community.

KINDNESS

I respect other people's views but object to being told what I should believe.

One part of life that seemed completely out of my control when I was younger, and in stark contrast to my chosen path, was the pressure to attend church. This was not limited to Sunday mornings. My dad was a Catholic and I was being brought up as a Catholic, which included attending additional bible classes after church and during the week.

When we were on family holidays abroad, I was taken to Catholic mass regardless of the language in which it was delivered. Sometimes it was Greek, sometimes Latin, so of course I had no idea what was being said. Although this was the norm for me, it was still a massive frustration and I wished it wasn't necessary, particularly as I didn't really believe in any god. This fact didn't seem to make a difference to anyone.

The following experiences are not about religion at all, but about human behaviour and kindness, or lack of such. They underpin a small part of my reason for wanting to make people feel heard and to make a difference in the world.

Three occasions from the 1970s are imprinted on my mind.

When I was eight or nine, a nun at the Catholic convent school I attended from ages five to nine had a highly refined skill for reducing girls to tears at every given opportunity. On this occasion, she spoke particularly unkindly to a very shy girl in my class, about her weight and apparent inability to play the recorder. This may seem like almost nothing to many, but it is still so clear in my mind and had a huge impact on me. I felt such sorrow for my classmate and importantly I felt totally helpless.

Another of my friends received the same treatment for her poor eyesight and inability to read to an expected standard. I met this girl years later and she told me she had been diagnosed as dyslexic. Of course, this was not considered in the 1970s but kindness would have made a huge difference regardless.

I found these incidents quite upsetting as I had been unable to stop them from happening and felt hurt on behalf of my friends. As I grew up, I felt a strong need to be in control of situations where injustice was a factor – a trait that still gets me in trouble today.

Around two years later, I was regularly being sent to an after-school religious group. The person running the group spoke to me about the recent death of my grandpa, whom I loved very much. I was desperately upset and wanted reassurance that he would be happy now, having suffered a long illness. Instead, I was quite directly informed that, as my grandpa had not been religious, he would go to hell! An interesting comforting technique, I thought.

Having said all that, I did enjoy midnight mass every Christmas Eve. This was always an exciting and magical time with the additional bonus element of a very late bedtime. I loved Christmas as everything felt different somehow. The family seemed more relaxed and at ease and there was a sense of togetherness that, although I would have denied it at the time, I craved more than anything.

Leaving out my pillowcase for Santa was still associated with warm, safe feelings, full of anticipation, even though Santa had left the picture years beforehand. From a wellbeing perspective, it is helpful to reflect on times, smells or sounds that conjure up warm and pleasant feelings.

I don't meditate but often use the sense of touch, the sound of songs, and well-loved smells to lift my mood. I particularly love the smell of fresh grass. The smell of vanilla, however, is totally nauseating to me unless it's very cold and in a bowl with a spoon.

My life experiences up to that point had, to all intents and purposes, made me both stronger and needier at the same time. I seemed to lurch from confident outgoing behaviour, often seen as arrogant by those around me, to a needy person confiding all my perceived inadequacies and self-esteem issues to my diary.

I KNEW IT!

1982 was a pretty ordinary year to start with, until the time we returned from our family summer holiday. By then, my brother had left home. As always, I was sitting on my own watching our little portable black and white TV, feet defiantly up on the TV table, which was actually an old chest of drawers. Mum came in and asked me to switch the TV off.

I begrudgingly did so; impatiently turning to her with a face of teen thunder.

"Your dad and I have decided to separate for a while," she said very quietly.

"How annoying," I thought, giving no obvious response whatsoever to my anguished mother.

It had finally happened.

My mum left the room soon after, having received no feedback from her obstinate and uncommunicative daughter; leaving me to consider the repercussions of this news.

> *"Dear Diary… I found out today that Mum and Dad are splitting up! This means they lied to me when they told me this wouldn't happen, **and** we will have to move house again!"*

Years later, I was mortified at my teen self's insensitivity to the situation, particularly as I had to have the same conversation with my own daughter in 2000 when splitting from her dad.

My daughter gave a similar response to me when I tried to talk to her, so I felt suitably paid back. I do feel sympathy for my younger self, though. As the wandering nomad I had been forced to be, I felt driven to protect my real feelings just to get by.

So back to the next house move…My mum owned a terraced house which had been divided into two flats many years before. My brother had been living in the top flat and used to pay me to clean for him which was a great arrangement for me. He hated cleaning. I loved cleaning and needed money to buy stuff. I now know that 'stuff' isn't going to make anyone happy but at the time 'stuff' was the elixir of life.

After my parents split, my Mum and I moved to the flats. My brother moved out to go travelling and I, of course, demanded the top flat for myself.

I was so hormonal and angry that my poor mother had no hope of controlling me really, so my wish was granted and many a party followed.

Now, as a mother myself, I am more than a little horrified at my behaviour. I was quite vile at times and knowing what I now know, I can see that my hormones were my main driving force for everything.

Christmas of 1982 was a dismal affair, with my parents trying to be normal amidst a divorce. It was traumatic for all concerned, but my teen passion for the pop group Japan helped to ease the sadness a little as I listened to their LP on my record player. They were my idea of dreamy.

This was also the year I popped a toe into the pescatarian life-style and had my first pescatarian Christmas dinner which was a less than wholesome packet prawn curry. This phase lasted around three months as the pescatarian meal options in the 1980s were not hugely appealing and I lost interest.

I have now been pescatarian again for over seven years and find it suits me well for many reasons, including my gut health and my love of animals. Apologies to the fish I still eat, but I'm old now and I need the omega-3 and all those essential minerals.

At that time, I should have been revising for my 'O' levels, which became GCSEs in 1986, but I had too much else going on to be bothered with that and I have already told you about my revision skills.

With newly dyed purple hair and raging hormones, I exuded mixed signals to everyone around me. No one was safe from my erratic state of mind, it seemed.

"Dear Diary... I am getting bored of writing a diary. This may not last."

Future me would smile at this comment when I finally stopped writing a diary nineteen years later. It had become increasingly clear that writing a diary had a positive psychological effect on me and I relied upon the support it offered. Much later in life, I was able to reflect that the mere action of writing down my feelings was a huge comfort during troubled times and I highly recommend it. No-one in the world knew me as well as my diary; partly because I didn't allow anyone to burrow under my external self-esteem shield for fear of being torn away from them.

When I met Roger, he took the time to get to know me better than anyone and has given me the confidence to let people in, beyond that shell. Less than a week after meeting him, I stopped writing a diary and have never felt the need to restart. It was a conscious decision that I didn't need a diary any longer. I now have different coping mechanisms for challenging times and a few years ago, I shredded all my diaries. They no longer represent who I am, and it was time. That was fun. Very empowering.

Side Note

I dislike the word 'journalling' as it's so much more than that.

Collins Dictionary states that it is *"the practice of keeping a journal or diary, especially to express one's thoughts"*

(Harper Collins Publishers 2024 - https://www. collinsdictionary.com/dictionary/english/journalling)

My own diary was my confidante, my friend and my paper psychologist.

When you put your thoughts down on paper, you're addressing how you feel and acknowledging those feelings by making them tangible. You make them easier to reach and to deal with.

Paper and pen work better than electronics in such cases as this requires the connection of letters by combining the use of your brain and motor skills; further activating your cognitive abilities.

This process takes the power out of your less positive thoughts, which is important in being able to move forward. It helps remove the mind clutter caused by overthinking everything during peri and post-menopause.

And who doesn't love the opportunity to buy more stationery?

LAYERS

When we were in our late thirties, Roger noted that I am a three-layered personality.

Layer one:

When people first meet me, they see the life and soul of the party. *'She's fun'* they think.

Layer two:

My barriers are up, and my insecurities make for someone often perceived as spiky or harsh.

Layer three:

For those who persevere and are permitted to reach this stage, I am considered loyal, loving, fun and empathic.

I have worked very hard over the past twenty-plus years to become more self-aware and layer two has become less prevalent but, when it is there, it's usually a response to external influences.

We all need a layer two for protection sometimes.

You are also a multi-layered person even if you don't realise it. You can decide how much of yourself you share. I share intimate details about myself with the intention of normalising the experiences of my clients and community and hopefully making them smile, but however, you feel, you will never be the only one feeling this way.

It is worth considering how you're perceived and whether it's correct *or* whether you even give a flying hoot!

Menopause is rubbish, hilarious and a privilege and I often find humour in the ridiculousness of our bodies as well as the practical solution to the problem. I'm in awe of, amused by, and often frustrated with our bodies and all they bring along, but it took me a long time to grow into myself. To help you progress during your menopause years, I prefer to offer practical guidance with integrated mindset support. You hardly even notice the mindset element, but I promise you it's there.

Chapter Two

WHAT IS MENOPAUSE?

The topic of menopause can seem complicated and over-whelming, so let's get down to some basics. When you know the basics about menopause, you can then understand the process of how to feel well and get the most from those hormones that seem to be out to get you.

Many of the women I meet have little knowledge of their own current or future menopause, which leaves them vulnerable to being fed fake facts and scaremongering, which in turn breeds fear and anxiety. Not what you need when you're already anxious and fearful.

Even if you already know about menopause, it is worth a reminder of the basics and definitely worth a read if you don't.

Early references to menopause have been difficult to find but we do know that Aristotle referred to the age of a woman at menopause as forty. This is out of context of course, but even today we are surrounded by an overwhelming flow of misinformation and misplaced advice from medical experts on topics such as…

What happens to our bodies during perimenopause?

When might we expect menopause to start?

and

How long will menopause last?

It is documented that women in Ancient Greece at this life stage were considered 'bewitched' I quite like the thought of being considered bewitched, but maybe that's just me.

PERIMENOPAUSE AND MENOPAUSE

Here's my definition:

Perimenopause is the beginning of the end of your fertile years, not the beginning of *the end!*

It is the time when your hormone levels start to decline but before you completely stop your periods.

It really is a privilege to even experience perimenopause. In the eighteenth century, women often died by the age of around thirty-three. In general, they would have had their children and not have had the opportunity to even reach perimenopause.

For this reason alone, I view menopause as a positive as the alternative is not hugely appealing. We are so fortunate to now be able to live longer, healthier lives.

What's Going On?

Estrogen, progesterone and testosterone levels fluctuate up and down as you head towards full menopause and your ovaries stop doing their thing. This phase could last for over twelve years. Yes! Twelve years.

Most of the time when we talk about menopause we are referring to our estrogen levels, as estrogen is paramount to our wellbeing. However, there are actually three main hormones to consider: estrogen, progesterone and testosterone. I discuss the other two later, but for now, let's focus on estrogen.

Both men and women produce estrogen, but women produce much higher levels. Depending on the stage of her cycle, a woman's levels can range from around 110-1400 pmol/L or higher, whereas a man's levels will range from around 30-180 pmol/L.

MENOPAUSAL SYMPTOMS

The reference to symptoms a little later on, and at the end of this chapter include the most impactful symptoms based on my professional experience. I have outlined these in more detail.

There will be symptoms that you had no idea were even connected with perimenopause. You may have thought these were just quirks that you alone had to deal with or were told it's just part of getting older. I do not want this to be something you accept.

What Can You Expect from Perimenopause?

'In The Old Days…'

Gone are the days of older women talking about *'The Change'* in hushed tones behind closed doors.

Well, you'd think so, wouldn't you? In reality, we still have a long way to go. Talking about menopause is still painfully awkward for many, and just not an option for some. Even saying the words vagina or vulva can bring many people out in hives.

I, of course, say these words a lot, if only to normalise them for everyone else. Maybe you do too. One doctor recently referred to his female patient's vagina as her 'lady parts'.

I have no words to say about that. I think you know what I *want* to say.

I hear from women in their sixties, seventies and eighties who are still dealing with debilitating symptoms such as anxiety, low mood or vaginal discomfort. Many of these women have no idea what has happened or why, as they have often been led to believe that once their periods stop and they are post-menopausal, their symptoms should also stop. If the symptoms don't stop they are told this is just something to accept.

PERIMENOPAUSE: AGE IS JUST A NUMBER

Under Forty

Perimenopause isn't just for older ladies you know. *Wait… what?* I hear you cry.

Many people are still telling women they're too young to be perimenopausal even when they are over forty-five and sometimes over fifty! My eyes roll back in my head every time I hear this.

FACT:

You can become perimenopausal before the age of forty; known as premature perimenopause, depending on your medical situation.

Your health history is relevant for many reasons, such as a family history of premature or early menopause, medication or prior surgery which can all affect your hormones.

It is also evidenced to be more likely you will become perimenopausal at an earlier age if you have had IVF treatment(s).

I was thirty-seven when I became perimenopausal but of course, I had no idea.

Forty to Forty-Five

When you begin perimenopause between the ages of forty and forty-five, this is called early perimenopause but is not all that unusual.

FACT:

The process of perimenopause can last for over twelve years and the average age of full menopause in the UK is fifty-one. We can deduce with simple maths that it would be quite usual to start perimenopause at age forty; therefore, if you have symptoms at this age don't accept being told that you're too young.

Forty-Five Plus

Even though this is the most common age to start perimenopause, some women are still told they can't be perimenopausal as they're under fifty.

FACT:

This is not even logical. It shows a lack of understanding of hormones and maths. If you fall into this age bracket, you have neither a premature nor an early perimenopause but may still have a problem accessing support and practical guidance.

MENOPAUSE

Menopause is often confused with perimenopause as we've been given the impression that menopause refers to the whole process; where in fact, menopause is the stage of our development that follows the perimenopause stage.

I prefer to view it as a stage of development, in the sense that we now live longer, healthier lives and are fortunate enough to have the opportunity to manage symptoms that our ancestors could not.

The official line is that menopause is the point when you haven't had a period for a full twelve months. All that time after is known as post-menopause. Of course, you can look back and pinpoint the time when you became post-menopausal but it's difficult to assess when your last period occurred until time moves on a little.

BLOOD TESTS

Many women are told that they must have blood tests to be considered perimenopausal.

One of my clients was told by her doctor that she couldn't have HRT until her blood tests confirmed she was perimenopausal. This particular woman was fifty-six and had not had a period for four years, which was a clear indication of post-menopause but who are we to muddy the water with facts?

If you are over forty-five, hormone blood tests to assess peri-menopause are not necessary as you should be assessed based on your symptoms and health history. However, any blood tests to establish your hormone levels will need to be taken at least twice with around a six-week gap between each test to gauge fluctuations, rather than a one-off result which would essentially be a snapshot of your hormones at that date and time in your cycle[1].

A Little Note Regarding Doctors...

I have great sympathy for the pressure put upon doctors regarding assessing perimenopause and prescribing HRT, but the knowledge I am passing on to you is not new news. It is based upon experience, evidence and scientific study.

We are fortunate to have the science in place to help us thrive during perimenopause and menopause, but this is only useful if we are taken seriously and treated with empathy and kindness. I am a huge promoter of women advocating for their own health, but success also requires a collaborative approach from clinicians.

It is clearly better to empower women with safe and regu-lated HRT, if this is what they want and need, than it is to offer drugs that will not solve the underlying issue, or worse,

---

1. This applies to assessing whether you are perimenopausal and not on HRT. It does not apply when establishing whether you are absorbing your HRT effectively, as a single blood test can give a good guide in this case.

to deny the problem exists, resulting in further time-wasting doctor's appointments to deal with ongoing menopause symptoms.

Share but Don't Compare

Of course, each of us is different and we can't tell exactly when someone will become perimenopausal, but there are clear indicators to look out for, with symptoms and hormone history being the main ones. It is really helpful to talk to your friends about your symptoms, but aim to share not compare, as your experience will be very different from that of others.

If your friend says she is 'sailing through it' then firstly, she might not have taken her long-term health into account and secondly, it's likely that your body and desires for your health are different from those of your friend. Never feel guilty or judged for wanting to do things your way.

I'm a bit of nag about this as we are all so different in our experiences of peri and post-menopause and our symptoms are affected by our lifestyles, stress levels, health histories and so much more.

I *love* HRT but it's not my role to force you to take it. My role is to give you the facts, talk about your situation and discuss your concerns and questions; then you're ready to make the best decision for you.

Pregnancy and Menopause

If you are sexually active with a man and you have a functioning uterus and ovaries, you need to use contraception until you're fully menopausal, unless you are prepared for the possibility of welcoming a little bundle of joy during your peri and early menopausal years!

If you're under fifty, you're no longer considered fertile two years after your last period. If you're over fifty, this is one year after your last period.

SYMPTOMS

You can find a longer list of symptoms further into this chapter, but a 2022 survey of my HRT group with around twenty-five thousand members at that time, identified the following symptoms as the most problematic.

- Exhaustion
- Weight gain
- Brain fog
- Heavy or erratic periods
- Low mood
- Anxiety
- Digestive issues
- Low libido

Exhaustion

This debilitating symptom can result from disturbed sleep, low mood, erratic periods and any of the other symptoms, to be honest! Many women feel more than just tired due to the hormone fluctuations.

I often liken this feeling to the plug having been pulled from your energy socket. It is quite unique and can be debilitating. I experienced this symptom quite severely and at times found it a challenge to get to the end of the day without a snooze. I even had to take time off work and many women leave work altogether when they feel they just can't cope.

What to Do

HRT will help to kick that into touch; however, you should also develop a regular and good sleep routine. Try to exercise two or three times a week as a minimum, but not just before bed or you'll be wide awake and unable to settle.

Try eating smaller meals and go for the grazing approach as this can keep energy levels up, whilst avoiding the bloating we can experience from larger meals. Try not to get too warm at night and let a bit of fresh air into the bedroom if you can.

Weight Gain

This topic is really big in the menopause community. I'll be honest with you; I tend to bat this one away a lot as it is often focused on people telling you that HRT makes you fat and focuses on swapping diet tips, so weight becomes a very different conversation, taking us away from the facts and positivity of HRT.

There is a whole book to be written about this topic alone but here are the key points from my mind palace of menopause and HRT.

My message is mostly about how *menopause* affects weight rather than how HRT affects weight. This is because HRT is not shown to be the cause of weight gain, but as always it is all about balance. I have previously put on weight purely due to my own symptoms, stresses, lack of exercise and less than ideal nutrition.

You may know of or remember women who seemed to become much rounder in the tummy area as they got older, but they just put up with it. You may think you have to just put up with it too. You don't. That extra roundness is down to your body working harder to cope with the hormonal changes.

As estrogen levels decline, your body starts to store fat in the abdomen area and if you feel particularly stressed about it all, the body produces more of the stress hormone cortisol, which further increases the fat production. (thanks body!)

What to Do

Definitely take more exercise. It is best to look at weight-bearing exercise. I started weight training at the age of fifty-six so no excuses. Pilates and yoga are great for overall health.

Some studies show that exercise, especially in the cold, increases our fat-burning friends – muscle and brown fat. Brown fat creates heat which burns calories and helps to regulate sugar, so stay active… (*Says me who is currently crouched over my laptop in the shape of a croissant!*) The more we exercise the more we strengthen our muscles and bones and increase the nerve-related protection around our joints which reduces the risk of hip and other fractures.

During peri and post-menopause, you may move less because you feel tired and low along with your joints becoming a bit stiffer, which means you burn less energy. The motivation to get out and about is challenging when you feel rubbish and it can take time for your body to adjust to a new HRT regime, so settling time is paramount.

It is less than helpful to be told you cannot have or must stop taking HRT as you are overweight. This is not true anyway as gels, patches and sprays do not increase blood clot risks but plenty of non-HRT medications do. It feels like a punishment to women who are vulnerable and struggling to be told to do better if they are to be 'rewarded' with HRT.

Nutrition is important too and in Chapter Eleven you will find some important nutrition tips to get you started. You can't assume that you can continue to eat what you were able to eat before perimenopause. Your body is not the same as it was, but it can still be healthy and strong.

You may develop some additional intolerances affecting digestion and your body will need different amounts of proteins and fats. Try to eat smaller portions as you probably need less food than you used to. Make sure each portion is full of nutritious food that will protect your health as well as help your weight. Reduce your intake of sugar and processed foods which are enemies of weight loss and more likely to increase abdominal fat, which is the less friendly fat.

The changing hormones during menopause can affect the way we store fat around the middle where men traditionally store their fat, rather than on the hips, hence that rounder tummy area. Fat around the middle is associated with heart disease, diabetes and liver disease so it's worth avoiding if you can.

We also lose muscle by around eight percent every ten years after forty. Muscle is more metabolically active, which means it burns more energy, so it helps us lose weight even when we're sitting.

More muscle = More calories burned = Weight loss

That's some easy maths.

There is some evidence that lower levels of fat-burning brown fat may contribute to the middle-age spread too. This is an area being heavily researched. Studies also show that we may need around two hundred fewer kcals each day than we did in the past…and it's very easy to ingest two hundred kcals without noticing it. One large wine will be almost enough.

Estrogen has a vasodilation impact, which means it helps the arteries to widen, therefore reducing blood pressure. The low/no estrogen during peri and post-menopause means we have an increased risk of heart disease. Choose fresh fruit and veg, oily fish, nuts, whole grains and white meat over red to reduce your overall risk. Of course, by adding your hormones back via a good HRT regime, you will help reduce that risk even further.

Address areas that cause you anxiety and stress as cortisol encourages abdominal fat stores.

And you guessed it…consider **HRT** which is not evidenced to cause weight gain and may actually prevent that abdominal fat from building up.

Do try to relax about HRT and remember that it's there to help you if you can let it do its job.

Brain Fog

This symptom can be quite scary, and you may feel that you're losing your mind.

Our hormones affect so much of what we do, and our brain is no exception. We have several estrogen receptors in our brain, so when our hormone levels are fluctuating or low, this has an impact on our memory and ability to concentrate.

What to Do

As you might expect, I recommend talking to your doctor about your symptoms and raising the topic of HRT but it's also important to consider any relevant lifestyle changes. Make sure you have good quality sleep and avoid too much alcohol and caffeine. HRT is very good, but it's not magic!

Heavy or Erratic Periods

In the early stages of perimenopause, you may experience more or less frequent periods but as time progresses, they'll space out and become fewer and lighter.

It is quite confusing to know where you are with it all and many women report that the worst element of this is the not knowing. Not knowing when or if a period is coming makes it really difficult to prepare and plan.

In my late thirties I had no idea I was perimenopausal, so I was in for a shock as I came down the escalator in a well-known department store and felt a gush as my unexpected period started with some force. I managed to cover my lower half with my jacket but had to wait what seemed like ten years until I reached the end of the escalator and then ran back up the other side to the toilets upstairs. Let's just say that the shopping trip ended there. Fun times.

What to Do

Please speak to your doctor if you experience any of the following:

- Extremely heavy bleeding that requires a change of pad or tampon every hour.
- Bleeding that lasts seven days or more for no known reason.
- Unexpected bleeding that occurs more frequently than every three weeks.

It is likely to be totally fine, but you need to check for any nasties like fibroids, cysts or anything sinister. Avoiding a worry never made it better.

Low Mood

If you become irritable or are feeling sad, down or maybe lacking in joy and motivation when you used to be more upbeat, this is one of the indications of declining or fluctuating estrogen levels, especially if you have other symptoms as well.

Depression is more serious and can lead to dark thoughts and despair so if this is you, it's vital that you seek support as soon as possible to receive the treatment you need.

What to Do

This may simply be a case of needing to start a course of HRT but it's important to discuss how you feel with the doctor.

Anti-depressants are not usually the first line treatment for perimenopausal symptoms, but they are sometimes necessary in addition to HRT if you are clinically depressed for non-hormonal reasons or have become very low.

FACT:

If you have ever suffered from Post Natal Depression (PND), you are statistically more likely to struggle with low mood symptoms during perimenopause. This isn't a reason to worry. It is merely a reason to be aware of your own body and how you feel.

Anxiety

As with low mood and depression, if you feel anxious or low and this is unusual for you, it may be perimenopause related. However, there are several conditions that could also make you feel this way so it's important to speak to the doctor, then they can eliminate other medical or psychiatric conditions.

What to Do

If you're particularly anxious or having panic attacks, you may benefit from an antidepressant even if you are on HRT.

You may feel a lot better on the right HRT regime, so shouldn't be prescribed antidepressants alone for anxiety related to perimenopause, and these will not be the first option to try unless your doctor feels you are in crisis and need the support.

Digestive Issues

The gut is important in our overall health and relies on estrogen just like the rest of our body. The change in hormone levels can slow down your digestion, start new digestion issues or exacerbate current issues.

The types of problems you might experience are constipation, diarrhoea, bloating, wind, nausea or acid reflux. All highly annoying and unwanted symptoms. You may have these symptoms already and they become worse during perimenopause, or you may experience new digestive challenges.

What to Do

Make sure you speak to your doctor about any new digestion problems, including and especially blood in your poop.

You should be looking at your poop you know. I don't mean you should settle in for an evening of it but a quick look to check for changes and blood is definitely a good thing.

Low Libido

You may stop having sex due to lack of interest or because you start to associate it with pain, discomfort and anxiety.

A healthy sex drive is a challenge when trying to get back to normal and it can put a strain on a relationship as you try to find a solution. Many relationships end due to the change in desire to have sex, which is often totally avoidable.

What to Do

Sex drive in women is complex. As a starting point, I suggest getting your testosterone levels checked as low testosterone affects both energy levels and sex drive.

MENOPAUSE SYMPTOMS LIST

I will precede this by saying that there are many variations of this list depending on who you speak to, and individual interpretations of symptoms vary. As always, I like to simplify things, so I have listed the most common ones.

You may have all, some or none of these symptoms but you can still be perimenopausal either way.

To be honest, you're unlikely to experience all the symptoms, but let me reassure you that you do not need to put up with feeling rubbish, however many symptoms you recognise in yourself.

- Hot flushes
- Night sweats
- Cold chills
- Sore breasts
- Headaches
- Digestive issues including bloating, constipation or diarrhoea
- Bleeding gums
- Inability to concentrate
- Vertigo
- Dizziness or feeling faint
- Facial hair
- Clammy skin
- Heart palpitations where your heart beats quickly or the beats feel stronger
- Low mood
- Depression

- Irritability
- Mood swings
- Erratic periods
- Electric shock feelings
- Itchy skin
- Leakages or other bladder issues
- Poor memory
- Lack of focus
- Brain fog
- Dry, itchy, sore or irritated vagina
- Aching joints or muscles
- Tense muscles
- Ringing or buzzing in the ears; known as tinnitus
- Weak fingernails
- Bad breath
- Changes in body odour
- Tearfulness
- Poor quality sleep or insomnia
- Fatigue experienced as feeling overly tired or lacking in energy
- Anxiety including feeling nervous for no reason
- Allergies
- Burning tongue or mouth
- A general lack of joy for life or interest in doing things
- Pins and needles
- Breathing problems

CHAPTER THREE

THE HISTORY OF HRT

THE HISTORICAL MISTREATMENT OF WOMEN

I am going to throw this into the mix at this stage as it's important to acknowledge that we are still experiencing much of the same attitude to female health as we have done for hundreds of years. I am all for a light-hearted approach, but that doesn't mean I find some of the treatment of women acceptable.

Throughout history, women have been dismissed as 'hysterical' or side-lined when voicing their needs.

In 2020 I wrote an article on the Misdiagnosis and Mistreatment of Perimenopausal Women from the Nineteenth Century to Modern Day. You can download that article on the following link or drop me a line on:

support@menoausalnotmad.co.uk and you'll receive the link.

https://www.menopausalnotmad.co.uk/wp-content/uploads/2024/04/2024-The-Misdiagnosis-Mistreatment-of-Women-19th-Century-Today.pdf

I can't believe that I still need to do what I do every day! I should be out of work after all the available menopause education of the past years.

Why, oh why, are we still trying to dispel the long-ago debunked study which stopped so many women being prescribed life-changing HRT? You'll learn more about that study further into this chapter.

I still regularly hear from women who are treated poorly regarding symptoms.

Here are just a few examples:

"Why would you need a libido now? You're over fifty and you've had your family."

"You can't expect to feel like you did when you were younger. It's normal to feel like you do as your age."

"You should just give up work now really."

And in my humble opinion, the worst I have ever heard:

"Ok, I'll let you have some HRT to improve your libido as I feel sorry for your husband."

Just let that statement sink in for a minute. And breathe.

Over half the population of the world will experience menopause, and this has a huge health impact.

The reduction in hormones makes it twice as likely that a woman will develop dementia compared with a man. She is also three times more likely to develop osteoporosis and her risk of heart disease significantly increases.

Even with the research and updates available, many people still don't understand that modern HRT does not have the same increased risks as the older options.

In May 2024 we finally saw some formal acknowledgment of something that I and many other HRT campaigners have known for years: The Women's Health Initiative (WHI) study of 2002 was not correct.

The WHI study and associated press releases essentially ruined and prematurely ended the lives of thousands of women with leaked and unverified data, feeding us headlines such as, *"HRT gives you breast cancer!"*

This led to many thousands of women being told they could not have or could no longer have HRT, and we have spent all the years following that, clawing our way back to some sense.

And on that note, here are some up-to-date facts:

- HRT reduces all-cause mortality (death) by 30%.
- HRT reduces the risk of diabetes by 30%.
- HRT reduces the risk of osteoporosis by half.
- HRT reduces the risk of heart disease by half.

Even though I am not a numbers person, let's be honest, those are significant numbers!

You can find up-to-date information on:

www.themenopausecharity.org and my own site www. menopausalnotmad.co.uk

THE TIMELINE OF HRT

The following timeline shows how we have been brought to the point of demonising our hormones.

The resulting gaslighting of women and disregard for the facts and overall benefits of hormone replacement has caused more damage than has ever been documented. Possibly you too have felt or still do feel, that HRT is bad because you've heard it said so often.

Without judgment, I hope you will soon feel differently. Even if you choose not to take HRT when you are peri or post-menopausal, you will be able to make that decision for your own reasons, rather than because of false information, scaremongering or an inability to access it.

1960s

Estrogen-only HRT was successfully used to treat menopausal symptoms.

1970s

It was found that estrogen-only HRT in women with their uterus still in place hugely increased the risk of endometrial cancer, and many women very tragically died as a result. This led to progesterone being introduced to stop this happening. This is now known as combined HRT.

Estrogen thickens the uterus lining (the endometrium), and progesterone thins it again. This balance is key as an over-thickened endometrium can increase the risk of endometrial cancer.

1980s

The advantages of HRT were seen and widely promoted.

1991

The Women's Health Initiative (WHI) was set up

2002

The WHI trial results were prematurely leaked to the media. This was a pivotal point in HRT history.

Combined HRT prescriptions were stopped almost immediately, but for some reason estrogen-only HRT continued to be prescribed for two more years for those women who had no uterus.

2004

Estrogen-only HRT was also stopped due to stroke fears. The result was over twenty years and counting, of fear and confusion for women and doctors regarding the use of HRT.

BEFORE THE WHI STUDY RESULTS:

Female Heart Health Study 1989-1993

The first major cardiovascular (CV) health trial in women studied 875 women aged 45-64 in the first ten years post-menopause.

The main aim was to establish the effect of HRT on the risks of stroke or heart attack.

The only estrogen being used was conjugated equine estrogen. This is an estrogen made from horses' urine, called Premarin in the UK (Prempro in the US). This is not the same as the newer body identical options we have today, although this product is still available.

Even so, the results evidenced that with use of just Premarin, there was a twenty-three percent *reduced CV risk.*

When using Premarin *plus* natural progesterone; there was still a nineteen percent *reduced CV risk* and Premarin plus *synthetic* progesterone (taken every day or in a cycle) gave a five percent *reduced risk.*

So, although the benefits were less for the women who also took progesterone rather than estrogen alone, the CV risks were reduced with HRT, even when using the older style versions.

FACT:

Coronary heart disease (CHD) is the leading cause of death in women. It was evidenced before the WHI study that HRT reduced the risk of CHD by **fifty percent.**

WHAT WAS THE WHI STUDY?

This study of 160,000 women was primarily set up to assess CV risks with assessment of fractures as a secondary outcome. Assessment of breast cancer was merely a 'safety outcome': It was not the main reason for the study.

Women who had recently become menopausal were excluded as those findings were considered to be already clear. *Seventy percent of the participants were between sixty and eighty years old.*

This key point warped all the data.

The average age of the participants was sixty-three and a half years and twelve years post-menopausal.

Sixty-three is significantly older than the most common age of menopause, which is fifty-one, so, the comparison is already warped as older women have an increased risk of breast cancer and heart disease, regardless of taking HRT or not.

Relative Versus Absolute Risk

The risk factors are worth clarifying to make the whole picture clearer.

In the WHI study the breast cancer risk was identified as four in every one thousand women who were on the placebo (who had no HRT).

When estrogen and progesterone were added the number increased to five in every one thousand. This was stated as a twenty-five percent increase, which of course it is. In those terms it sounds scary but calculated as an 'absolute risk' this is only a 0.08% increase in risk.

This is still a low risk.

How was the Information Managed?

The usual protocol for managing data was not used. It was all but ignored and lead investigators were not consulted.

On 5 July 2002, just before the study was leaked, key specialists were attending a conference on HRT which included the renowned Professor John Studd. During that conference, Professor Studd proposed that HRT should be offered to women to take forever. *(Whoop whoop!)*

On 8 July 2002, the flawed and mismanaged data was leaked to the press. This was nine days before the clinical article was formally published and too late for any changes to be made. Lead investigators tried to change the publication and press release, but it was too late.

The overall data *actually* indicated the following:

- Although estrogen-only HRT in tablet form showed a small increased risk of blood clot issues, the data was considered to show a 'rare risk' which is so low as to be almost insignificant.
- Estrogen-only HRT was evidenced as reducing breast cancer risk.

I'll let you pause on that fact.

I will also add that if you read *Oestrogen Matters* by Medical Oncologist, Dr Avrum Bluming and Carol Tavris PhD, you will learn a lot about estrogen and how amazing it is. Doctor Bluming is highly regarded in his field and has personal family experience of breast cancer.

My favourite part of the book is the following:

> "If oestrogen were an important cause of breast cancer, we would expect rates of breast cancer to decline after menopause, when oestrogen levels naturally diminish. Instead, breast cancer rates increase."[2]

In 2024 Dr Bluming stated: "If the WHI had been transparent about their findings around breast cancer, there would have been 'minimal controversy, and women's health would not have suffered so dramatically over the ensuing decades."

---

2. Bluming & Tavris: Oestrogen Matters 2018, page 10

To return to the study which was prematurely stopped as there was some evidence of blood clot risk (but not in the lower risk fifty to fifty-nine age range) the beneficial signs of post-hysterectomy estrogen-only HRT were ignored. They were later shown as significant, in addition to a reduction in CHD in those starting HRT before age sixty.

Although the combined HRT of the time showed a small increased risk of blood clots, breast cancer and stroke with synthetic progesterones, the death rate was very low which meant that there was no increased risk of death.

It was clear, however, that there were also some benefits when looking at reduced risks of:

- Colon cancer
- Hip fractures
- Total fractures (this being the biggest benefit)
- Diabetes

WHAT HAPPENED WHEN THE WHI STUDY CAME OUT?

Women stopped taking HRT on a global scale. A Finnish study which ran from 1994-2009 charted the effects of stopping HRT.

It found that there was a statistically significant increase in strokes and blood clots in the first year after stopping HRT, probably due to the loss of support from estrogen via the vasodilatory effect. It is estimated that fifty thousand women died prematurely following surgical menopause after hysterectomy including the removal of ovaries, because they stopped or didn't start HRT.

I feel so sad for those women who died prematurely when there was a way to help avoid that.

An increase in fracture risk was identified as starting one year after stopping HRT and becoming statistically significant within five years.

My own mother was an example of this. She had to have a replacement hip within two years of being forced to stop her HRT at aged 64 years, and her other hip replaced a little later, where she had been fit and active until that point.

The WHI study resulted in all HRT products being badged as having the same risk level including vaginal topical estrogen, which showed zero risk in the WHI study and is still considered of no risk in 2024. We are, however, still regularly told by pharmacists, doctors and within the product leaflets, that we risk breast cancer when using low-dose topical vaginal estrogen to help tackle symptoms of genitourinary symptoms of menopause (GSM) which you may know as vaginal atrophy.

See Chapter Six on this topic for more guidance.

Studies at the time which were looking at the use of estrogen after a breast cancer diagnosis were stopped. This put back vital research for over twenty years.

Anti-depressants were prescribed in amounts directly relating to the drop in HRT prescribing, which in simple terms meant that HRT was replaced by anti-depressants.

I clearly remember being offered anti-depressants in the early stages of perimenopause and being told that I could not consider anything else until my periods stopped. This felt like a prison sentence to me, and I was not prepared to accept it as fact.

The Learns

The WHI study showed no positive or negative effect of HRT on CHD risk, but the results were flawed due to the age of the participants and cannot be applied to all women.

Further data clearly evidences a heart health benefit for younger women and women who are perimenopausal.

POST-MENOPAUSE AND HRT

Estrogen receptors respond differently after a long period with no estrogen. This fact cannot be ignored. We therefore need to ensure that younger and early perimenopausal women are offered the opportunity to reduce the risks of serious long-term health problems as soon as possible.

This is not to say that there is no point in starting HRT in later life (post-sixty or later than ten years post-menopause) but the benefits are fewer. Also, the approach needs to be sensitive to the fact that the body will need lower doses to adjust to the reintroduction of hormones.

Waiting until someone is post-menopausal before considering HRT is cruel, when access to treatment can help them feel better and have a healthier prognosis. I have a lot of clients and menopause community members who are over sixty and on HRT. They cannot believe the health and well-being improvements they experience.

FOLLOW-UP STUDIES

A 2017 review of the WHI study brought us the following data.

Use of Estrogen-Only HRT showed:

- A decrease in breast cancer risks.
- A decrease in breast cancer deaths.

Use of Combined HRT (estrogen and synthetic progesterone) showed:

- A small increase in breast cancer risk.
- No significant increase in breast cancer deaths.

Any increased risk of breast cancer with the synthetic progesterone used in the combined HRT tablet called Femoston is still not significant. Once again, not all HRT options are equal.

Progesterone

Utrogestan is a body identical progesterone tablet and has no increased risk of breast cancer within the first five years. Any increased risk is still low after five years.

SUMMARY POINTS

Women all have individual risk factors but after fifty years of HRT studies, there is still no conclusive evidence that HRT causes breast cancer.

Body identical combined HRT appears to have no effect on breast cancer risk. Any risk that exists is extremely small at one extra woman in one thousand every year.

Estrogen-only HRT seems to be protective.

The type of progesterone is important. Micronised is better, which in the UK is usually Utrogestan. In some other countries, Prometrium is often the equivalent but other equivalent brands are available.

> **Side Note**
>
> It is worth stating at this point that *Progesterone* is the name of the body identical product but *Progestogens* or *Progestins* are the synthetic versions of progesterone such as those in the combined patches, the contraceptive pill or many of the combined tablets. However, for ease of understanding I will refer to all three as *progesterone* within this book.

Blood Clot Risk

After all the data had been properly studied, the only significant risk identified was that of blood clots when taking the tablet form of HRT – but not with Utrogestan or Prometrium. This risk can be completely avoided by using transdermal estrogen via patches, spray or gel. However, there is evidence to indicate that some synthetic progesterones may slightly increase breast cancer risk.

One study stated that estrogen tablets have what is termed a 'double increased risk'. This is still only double a low risk. The risk is highest in the first year of taking it and it confirmed that transdermal estrogen has no increased blood clot risk.

Breast Cancer

It was clearly identified in all studies that there is no increased breast cancer risk with estrogen and when comparing the 12,304 women joining the WHI study with no previous HRT use, the breast cancer risk was exactly the same as the placebo.

With reference to breast cancer risks; I am not referring to those who have or have had estrogen receptor-positive cancers. However, even in these cases HRT is not evidenced to be the cause of the cancer, but caution is needed when considering introducing estrogen in such cases and expert clinical guidance is required.

Stroke Risk

In the WHI study, the risk of stroke in the fifty to fifty-nine age group was equal to that of the placebo group. Overall, the risk was increased with oral estrogen. As we know, the ages of participants were much higher in these groups, so they had a higher stroke risk factor anyway.

The Finnish study evidenced that taking any HRT regime at any age for less than ten years was associated with nineteen in one thousand *fewer* CHD deaths and seven in one thousand *fewer* stroke deaths.

Osteoporosis

We assume that significant bone degeneration is part of ageing, but this does not need to be the case! Menopause does lead to bone density loss and HRT is the only therapy considered to both prevent and treat this life-limiting problem. HRT is clearly evidenced to help in preventing fractures and to improve menopause symptoms.

It is heartening to read that HRT is recommended by the International Menopause Society (IMS) as first-line therapy for osteoporosis in those under sixty, within ten years of menopause. This is not to say it is ineffective in women over sixty who have been menopausal for longer, but the impact of the

HRT will be different. The key is to stop the degeneration in the first place.

Dementia

Estrogen supports our brain function.

It surprised me to learn that dementia is considered to be a disease of middle age (around the most common age of menopause), which can take twenty years to manifest itself and an early menopause can lead to increased dementia risk. This includes those who have had a surgical menopause or those with premature ovarian insufficiency (POI), a condition which means a woman's ovaries stop working before the age of forty.

HRT is key in such situations.

Links between HRT and brain function are quite controversial, and the trials are not easy to set up, but evidence seems to indicate that introducing estrogen within five years of menopause is beneficial. At this stage, it is not usual to use HRT purely for cognitive (brain) function other than for women with POI.

Data individually interpreted by Jane Pangbourne from *Newson Health Menopause Society (NHMS) update "20 years on from the WHI study"* 6th July 2022

WHAT NOW?

In 2024 we are seeing a lot of progression in menopause knowledge but still too much dismissal of needs and backward steps in this area. It is important we don't become complacent about our role in staying up to date.

Many doctors are not up to date on the correct HRT data and evidence, but there are lots who are very happy to learn and want to help you during peri and post-menopause. I view this to be a collaboration where we help doctors to help us. You know you best.

The NICE Guidelines on shared decision making (2020) outline how doctors should aim to work with their patients to form an individual plan.

You can view them on:

https://www.menopausalnotmad.co.uk/wp-content/uploads/2021/02/updated-decision-making-and-consent-guidance_pdf-84160128.pdf

It is personal choice, of course, but there is little evidence to suggest that HRT is harmful, and it offers some great health benefits to improve both quality and length of life. We know that lifestyle factors such as exercise, alcohol intake and weight are key to breast cancer risk and have much more of a negative impact on risk factors.

I for one will never stop replacing my hormones and will fight for as long as I can for women to do the same.

Update: 1ˢᵗ May 2024

"Among women below the age of sixty, we found hormone therapy has low risk of adverse events and [is] safe for treating bothersome hot flashes, night sweats and other menopausal symptoms" says study author Dr JoAnn Manson, chief of preventive medicine at Brigham and Women's Hospital. She also stated: *"This is a departure from the advice many women have been given in the past."*

This is another small step forward for the HRT message, although the word 'bothersome' is not one I would use, and it is important to also include women over sixty in the overall message.

Chapter Four

THE POWER OF THE BODY CLOCK

When I left school I had definitely not achieved my full potential, having decided a long time before that being academic wasn't to my advantage. I did not revise for my exams so left school with only a handful of 'O' levels.

In later years I founded and managed a government funded training company, helping long-term unemployed adults into work. The irony wasn't lost on me that I was coaching people on the benefits of putting effort into their studies to progress in life but had waited until my own adulthood to get my act together, and later retrain as a national assessor, verifier, and adult tutor.

I loved that role in the same way I love my role today. However, the inauthenticity of those in higher authority and in other organisations made it untenable for me to continue to help those most in need, so things needed to change. I am not one to sit around when things are not working, and I try to impart the same ethos onto everyone I meet.

If it works, do more of it.

If it doesn't work, change it.

If it makes you miserable, walk away with your head held high.

So… back to leaving school.

Even in teen mode, I realised I needed to get my shit together as I was keen to progress and grow. I had plans to change the world and, of course, I was fearless at that age.

I applied to attend beauty therapy college, purely because that was readily available and seemed like a good idea. It wasn't!

I didn't get in the first time I applied so went to another college to study more 'O' levels. I did no revision for anything. Even though I loved my psychology and biology classes, I failed both exams as I had no idea how to revise and way too much free time to party. Forgetting to check my exam paper properly before leaving the exam room subsequently resulted in disaster as I had missed a key section, resulting in a fail.

This was all a sliding doors moment for me as those qualifications would have put me on the road to a different future. However, I regret nothing, and I made the best of the situation I was in, as I still do with all challenges today.

I reapplied to beauty therapy college but notably, I dressed and acted like a completely different person, just to fit in at the interview. I was accepted but, unsurprisingly I hated the course. I do still have some hairdressing skills though if I ever need to earn a few extra pennies. You know where to find me.

Never try to be something you're not and never try to please others by sacrificing who you are.

Nearing the end of the first year in beauty therapy college, I had my first experience of what I now know to be anxiety. I felt very shaky on a regular basis and would break out in red blotches all over my face for no apparent reason. It's clear to me now that I was not doing the things that met my emotional needs.

Decision time came when I took my first-year massage exam, which I was carrying out on my tutor. I nailed the technical side of that. Go me!

However, my tutor's feedback was simple:

"Great technique Jane, but that was the quickest and least restful massage I have ever had."

Oops! A career review was required.

My sense of urgency and of getting the job done wasn't helpful in the beauty therapy world, so I left; much to the dismay of my poor mum who had spent a fortune on my equipment and books. Now I was in a pickle and my hormones were on the rampage. I was around eighteen at that time and a woman's hormones peak at around nineteen or twenty… fun times.

This was, I think, the first time in my life that I asked for help from an expert. I lived in Coventry so walked into town, straight into the careers office and asked for a careers interview.

It's odd that I still remember that interview after nearly forty years, but it was life changing.

The interviewer had only known me a few minutes but deduced in that time that I would flourish in a customer-focused environment and that I needed to be in control and busy, with lots of variety. I was an open book even in those days, it seems, and I'm a terrible liar.

I was in awe of his ability to get to the core of my needs within minutes. I pride myself on having honed a similar skill to help my clients today. He suggested I look at hospitality management and told me to apply to all the big hotel chains to see what responses I received.

I did as I was told which was quite unusual in itself, and quickly realised I needed to get back into education to re-train if I wanted to take over the world of hospitality. I was soon accepted onto a highly regarded hospitality management programme, putting me on the road to finding my feet as a useful adult.

Spoiler alert: I never did take over the world of hospitality but had a ball in the process.

I have already told you that I have an erratic mind and focus is a challenge, but I completed my programme, achieved my Diploma and packed my bags to move to a new job way up North, as assistant manager for what was then Berni Inns.

I think another book about my years in hospitality and retail management is called for. That is more a tale full of intrigue and some seriously dodgy behaviour from many of my employers and managers, but for now let's just say I held a number of management positions all over the country.

MARRIAGE

I got married for the first time in 1991 at age twenty-three.

I now know that I married that first time because all my friends were getting married. I was lonely living in London and my body clock was telling me I should be having children soon. In case you need telling, these are not good enough reasons alone to get married!

We are slaves to our hormones, but I knew deep down that I was not ready to be married with a family. However, my hormones had a different plan. When I was hoping to get pregnant, I clearly remember feeling slightly insane in my desire for that to happen.

Retrospectively, I know I have a disposition for high and low moods, so hormone fluctuations were a recipe for mood soup. On that note, menopause is fabulous as we no longer have those extreme hormonal fluctuations.

PARENTHOOD

I love my children above all else, but I found early parenthood really challenging, partly due to my hormones and their impact on my mood, but it was more complex than that and probably related to my own upbringing and neurodivergent brain.

When my now thirty-year-old daughter was born after eighteen hours of labour, an episiotomy and a poorly inserted epidural that numbed my legs but still allowed all the pain of labour, I felt all my personal insecurities come to rest on my shoulders.

Many new mums around that time were also clearly struggling, but it felt unacceptable to even raise the topic in a public environment and shameful to vocalise such worries for fear of judgment. Having spoken with several women who had children at the same time as me, it appears to have resulted in many being robbed of the joy of parenthood.

Post-natal care is better than it was in my day as we are so much more knowledgeable and the internet offers access to previously unavailable support, but, as with menopause, each new mum is different. We must never forget that. We must also remove the narrative that having a baby should be a total joy or you must be doing it wrong or be a bad parent.

Newsflash! - It's not always a joy and you're not a bad parent.

As with menopause, life becomes different with a baby and needs some adaptation, support and facts with a good dose of empathy.

The crash in estrogen and progesterone levels after giving birth can have a minor or much more significant impact on a woman. In my case, I experienced post-natal depression (PND) for a long time afterwards whilst running a business and trying to be the best mum I could be.

This made me fearful of having a second child so when my son was expected in 1998, I had already started to research hormone therapies and made a formal request for hormone therapy to be administered immediately after he was born. I was subsequently given six weeks of combined hormone therapy via injection then suppositories and it was transformative. I had a totally different experience with no low moods and no crash in hormones. My life was better with hormones.

In 2008 the Cochrane study on the use of such therapy for the prevention of PND concluded there were only minor improvements in some cases and caution was necessary with synthetic progesterones, but my own experience was very positive. Since then, in 2019 (updated in 2023) the Food & Drugs Administration (FDA) in the US have stated that hormone therapy plays a major role in avoiding PND.

Incidentally, there is also a decrease in estrogen when we breastfeed. Therefore, many women will feel perimenopausal during this time too.

If these symptoms last only for a short time and you're not too affected by them, it is worth knowing that it's a thing but there is no need to take any action. However, if you're struggling, seek advice from your doctor or health visitor.

I often see women who have completed their family and stopped breastfeeding but still feel symptoms months after. In my experience of working with thousands of women, this is not uncommon. I liken it to our body saying, *"Great! Kids all sorted. No need for those hormones any longer."* Of course, it's not quite like that but I like to imagine it that way.

CHAPTER FIVE

TO HRT OR NOT TO HRT

In this chapter, I want to outline some important HRT information and respond to key concerns about HRT. I will also outline the most common HRT options to help you discuss your own needs with your doctor.

I'm a huge advocate of hormones and HRT, based on personal and professional experiences. There is a vast amount of evidence of the benefits for our physical and mental well-being, both short and in the longer-term. Some unregulated menopause remedies are quite simply not safe, so please check before spending your time or money and impacting your health with anything unproven, and only use regulated HRT prescribed by your doctor.

I fully accept that not everyone wants to take HRT and a few women will not be able to do so due to increased health risks. My guidance is merely intended to enable you to make your own choice. Nobody can tell you that you should or should not take HRT. When you have facts and evidence, you can make an informed decision on how best to use HRT to achieve the best result for you.

There is a lot of misinformation on Google which is outdated, incorrect and based on flawed data. Please don't Google "Will

HRT give me breast cancer?" That will not bring up factual, up-to-date information and you'll never want to read about HRT again.

HRT: THE BASICS

As you consider whether HRT is the right choice for you (spoiler alert! It probably is), it's essential to understand the facts.

What is HRT?

HRT is designed to alleviate the symptoms and long-term health issues of peri and post-menopause.

It involves the introduction of estrogen (also spelt oestrogen), usually progesterone and sometimes testosterone, to make up for the decrease in natural hormone levels that occur as we age, or due to medical issues or surgical interventions such as a hysterectomy.

HRT helps to reduce often-debilitating, upsetting and uncomfortable symptoms of peri and post-menopause, as well as helping to reduce the risks of osteoporosis, heart disease and other unwanted health nasties. In my humble opinion, this long-term health element is key.

Very briefly and as a rule, estrogen in HRT helps to reduce the symptoms and the long-term health risks of menopause. Most of our cells have an estrogen receptor attached to them, so the low or fluctuating levels during menopause can upset the delicate hormonal balance, resulting in a host of symptoms.

Progesterone has many benefits. From an HRT perspective. Its main role is to reduce the risk of endometrial cancer by keeping the uterus lining thin when we supplement estrogen in our bodies. Estrogen thickens the uterus lining whilst progesterone keeps it thin, so they are a lovely team.

Forms of HRT

HRT comes in several forms: oral tablets, patches, gels and sprays.

The dose and form prescribed, will depend on your individual needs and preferences.

Doing It Naturally

Women often say they want to manage their menopause 'naturally'. Here are a few things to consider:

Regulated HRT, in most cases, replaces our missing hormones with natural plant-based hormones. This is the most effective option for most women and offers huge health-protecting properties.

For those who demonise HRT, I say that we wouldn't dream of telling a diabetic to try to manage without their insulin top-ups or expect someone with an underactive thyroid to just 'get on with it' minus their daily thyroxine. I rely on thyroxine to stabilise my own underactive thyroid and could not manage without it; and don't get me started on the fact that men can access Viagra over the counter when they want to!

Conversely, the huge array of unregulated alternative solutions to which you have access can be harmful and will possibly do little to help you in the long term.

I am not suggesting you shouldn't use or take any verified complementary therapies. There is often a great balance to be found between HRT and some complementary options so it's not an either-or situation.

We live longer than nature originally intended so we were not expected to need our hormones later in life. For that reason, they naturally decline as we age but if somebody tells you that menopause is a natural state and you should just accept it, they do not understand progress, science and wellbeing.

Breast Cancer

Let's touch again on the biggest concern for women created by the WHI Study. Although breast cancer is a devastating disease, many more women die of heart disease than breast cancer.

Part of this is due to the reduced heart protection we have as our estrogen levels drop, but additionally, women can feel so awful during perimenopause that they are unable to exercise, or don't eat as healthily as they might, resulting in an overall health decline, which has the knock-on effect of making them more susceptible to heart problems.

You are much more at risk of breast cancer if you don't exercise, if you drink more than two units of alcohol a day or if you're very overweight, but we don't see a breast cancer warning on a bottle of our favourite tipple, do we?

As outlined in Chapter Three, studies evidence that estrogen in HRT is not the reason for the very small increased breast cancer risk. It is thought that this risk is more likely to be due to synthetic progesterone such as that in combined HRT tablets or combined patches. This is not a reason to panic if you're on the synthetic products. They are still excellent HRT products, but you may decide to make a different decision, knowing this information, or you may be happy to accept the small risk.

The health risks are often higher with no HRT than any risks when taking it.

Colon Cancer

In 2022 Steven R Goldstein MD who was president of the British Menopause Society at that time, stated that HRT *reduces the risk of colon cancer and promotes a leaner body mass.*

This results in less chance of obesity which leads to a healthier body and longer lifespan.

MAKING IT WORK FOR YOU

Many women tell me they have no idea whether they even have symptoms of menopause as they are so used to feeling horrible or think it's normal to feel so different to how they used to feel.

Many also believe that HRT just doesn't work for them. In most cases, they have been given shoddy advice, or no advice at all, on how to take it properly. When we dig into the detail of what they need, it's usually fine. Adjustments are made, and they feel better. Simple!

I want to add that most newly introduced HRT regimes or changes may take some time to settle. You won't usually feel miraculously well after twenty-four hours. Some women are fortunate in that they see huge improvements after a very short time whilst others take a few weeks or months and may experience some side effects as their body adjusts to the new situation.

Side effects such as some ad hoc bleeds, feeling a little 'jittery', or experiencing sore breasts are quite usual and nothing to worry about. Estrogen can be responsible for all that. It has a job to do and reigniting your cells is a good thing. If you're peri or post-menopausal, your body will thank you for allowing it time to settle.

A person with a particular sensitivity to hormones needs a different approach. This can usually be established by looking at their health and hormone history. There is always a way. For example, when you were younger you may have experienced a very low mood just prior to your period. This would indicate some intolerance to progesterone, so it's worthwhile reading Chapter Eight on progesterone intolerance and PMDD.

HRT OPTIONS

Some of the terms used below might be new to you, but you don't need to learn everything about HRT. You only need to know the bits that apply to you.

Please do note that although the transdermal gel and Utrogestan tablets are considered 'gold standard' HRT, this does not indicate that all other HRT options are of a low standard as this is not the case.

When we talk about HRT in terms of menopause, we mean: Estrogen, Progesterone and Testosterone replacement, which are the three key hormones.

Body Identical

In the UK, when something is called 'body identical' this means it is made from natural plant-based ingredients and closely matches your natural hormones. All the estrogen products you will access via your clinical doctor in the UK will be body identical.

In the UK, body identical progesterone is usually the Utrogestan tablets and recently, another option called Gepretix has joined the party. These have no blood clot risk as they are considered to have improved bioavailability. To you and me this just means they are absorbed more easily into the body.

Bio Identical

When something is called 'bio identical' or 'compounded' this mainly refers to unregulated hormone products. It is not HRT that I would recommend, as a rule.

I will say that I have previously suggested a bio identical product to a client who was based in Dubai with no access to regulated HRT. She was really struggling, and I needed to help get her through until she could access something else.

Non-UK

Just to confuse you... in non-UK countries, body identical HRT is often referred to as bio identical, so, be mindful from which country you are accessing your HRT.

The body identical progesterone in the US and some other non-UK countries is usually Prometrium or its generic equivalent.

Synthetic

Synthetic progesterone is a chemical product made to imitate natural progesterone.

HOW IS HRT TAKEN?

HRT can be taken in a variety of formats. There are gels, combined patches, combined tablets, estrogen-only patches, estrogen-only tablets, and spray.

Patches, gels and spray are transdermal which means they enter the body via the skin. Transdermal options bypass your gut so there will be less likelihood of stomach issues and no blood clot risk. These are great, safe options but if your skin is like that of a rhino; while it's doing a great job of being skin by keeping stuff out, it's not great for absorbing your HRT.

I usually suggest starting with one of the transdermal options, then reassessing the absorption of your transdermal HRT after a few months.

Doses will be based on individual circumstances. 2024 guideline updates from the British Menopause Society (BMS) state that higher doses of progesterone are advised with higher doses of estrogen. This is specifically aimed at the management of unscheduled bleeding on HRT.

I understand the need for guidelines, but I find some of them very frustrating. The 'sheep dip' approach to prescribing HRT for women results in a lack of individualisation and a lot of anxiety and misery for women who are prescribed inappropriate doses of both estrogen and progesterone, when doctors apply the guidelines to all women.

Here is a flavour of your HRT options. Of course, it is not an exhaustive or prescriptive list.

Oestrogel (estrogen gel)

Comes in a pump dispenser and is relatively easy to use. It takes a few minutes to dry. As with other gel options, it requires around one and a half to two hours after application before bathing, showering or swimming to ensure it is well absorbed.

It is quite bulky to take on your overseas holiday if you only have hand luggage.

Sandrena Gel (estrogen gel)

This comes in little sachets and in different doses. Great size for travelling but a little fiddly to use. It dries quite well on the skin but leaves a tacky feeling. Only a very small amount is needed in comparison with Oestrogel as it is more concentrated.

You will use any estrogen gel every day; usually applying to the outside of your arms or the inside of your thighs

Progesterone

If you still have your uterus, you will need to take progesterone as well as estrogen to help protect your uterus lining from an increased risk of endometrial cancer. If you didn't take progesterone you would be at the same risk level as the women in the 1970s outlined in Chapter Three.

However, if you've had a hysterectomy you usually only need the estrogen element of HRT, and studies show that this can actually reduce your breast cancer risk.

On the other hand, it is not uncommon to be prescribed progesterone after a hysterectomy for other reasons. Many women feel the benefit of this hormone aside from the uterus health need.

The progesterone can be in the form of the Utrogestan tablet, which is body identical and very safe, or a Mirena coil which is synthetic but still a good option. Any risks associated with the synthetic progesterone in the Mirena coil are very low because the coil is inserted into the uterus so doesn't work across the whole body and only a small amount enters the blood stream.

There are also combined patches to which I refer a little further on in this chapter. These contain both estrogen and synthetic progesterone. However, your needs will be dependent on a number of individual factors, and therefore your dosage and regime of estrogen and of progesterone are going to vary. You'll either be on a cyclical/sequential regime where you'll usually still have periods and take a higher dose for half the month, or a continuous regime where you'll usually have been period-free for twelve months or more and take a lower dose but every day of the month.

Put simply, this means you'll either take progesterone for part of the month or you'll take it every day.

I had a hysterectomy in 2022 and have never taken progesterone since that day, but I am an all-or-nothing kind of gal.

I have never felt any different without it so for me there is no current need. I am always flexible with my own HRT regime and am happy to take it later if my body indicates a need.

Progesterone is mostly a relaxing hormone, unless you're intolerant to it, and may even help you to sleep as it can have a sedative effect. There are several reasons why you might be on a continuous regime of progesterone, including endometriosis, low mood when not taking it or heavy bleeds.

Many of my clients really struggle without it and I wish it were more widely accepted that some people need it just to be able to get to sleep or to function effectively. It may improve your aches and pains and help with your mood so if you have had a hysterectomy it's worth testing this out to see whether you do benefit from progesterone. If you've had a hysterectomy as a result of endometriosis, it is often advised to continue with your progesterone as it helps to avoid endometriosis regrowth.

Before you leave your doctor's surgery or end that call, remember to ask how you should take your HRT. Try not to arrive home and then wonder what to do with this new prescription.

Progesterone Creams

Some people will tell you that progesterone creams are effective for uterus protection. This is not the case. You must use the recommended progesterone options offered by your doctor when adding in estrogen.

Progesterone creams are mostly cosmetic and are apparently good for your skin. In some cases, they can help with early perimenopausal symptoms, without estrogen, but cannot be considered part of HRT.

Combined Patches

Evorel Sequi and Evorel Conti both contain 50mcg of estrogen. There are currently no other doses available in this combined patch. The progesterone in these patches is synthetic.

Patches are a great option, but some people find that they don't stick well or that the glue irritates their skin. For example: I am highly irritated by the Evorel brand but have no problem with the Estradot brand of patches.

It is worth trying different brands to see what works for you. You may also find a fluffy, sticky mark left on your skin when you remove each patch as your clothing can stick a little but some baby oil or similar will usually remove this.

I have tried all types of HRT over the years and now I love my patches. Although I get the sticky marks on my skin, it's a small price to pay for my sanity!

You will usually apply the patch to your bottom, hip, thigh or abdomen and change it twice a week, using one patch for three days and one for four.

Evorel Sequi

The Sequi (short for sequential) regime contains two types of patches: Evorel 50 (estrogen-only) and Evorel Conti (estrogen and progesterone combined).

You must use the patches in the right order to help your cycle to become regular. This means two weeks of Evorel 50 patches followed by two weeks of Evorel Conti patches.

You will usually have a bleed during your Evorel 50 weeks as you have removed the progesterone from your HRT for those two weeks. This signals to your body that it's time for a period.

Evorel Conti

The Conti (short for continuous) regime is a combined patch, and women take this regime for a few reasons.

You won't *usually* have a period or bleed on this regime, but it can take a while to settle. Even though you have probably been told the absolute opposite of this, there is no health risk associated with being on a continuous regime before you are post-menopausal. Many women are told that they 'have to have a bleed' and this is just not true. If you are taking your progesterone as directed, this will keep your uterus lining thin and no shedding is necessary.

It is obvious that there is a global lack of understanding of how hormones and HRT work when I hear almost every week that women are told *no* to continuous progesterone but instead they are prescribed the *continuous* progesterone of the Mirena coil or the *continuous* progesterone of the progesterone-only contraceptive pill.

Come on, people! Let's at least try to join the dots a bit.

Yes, there is an increased chance of ad-hoc and irregular bleeding whilst your body adjusts to a daily progesterone regime. However, for women who have mood issues with fluctuating hormones, excessive bleeding each month or endometriosis, for example, this regular progesterone can be a lifesaver. Once again, we are all different.

Estrogen-only patches

There are several brands of estrogen patches. The most common UK versions are Evorel, Estradot or Estraderm. They come in a range of doses.

If you decide to use these, and you have not had a hysterectomy, you must add in a progesterone option such as the Mirena coil or Utrogestan.

Estrogen spray

Lenzetto is the brand name of the estrogen spray. It is a good product as it generally absorbs well. I have a few clients who have struggled to absorb the gels and patches but seem to do well with the spray.

However, I am reluctant to recommend it to my community because women are often 'underdosed' due to a current lack of understanding of the dose equivalents.

The dose (at the time of writing) is clarified on page four of the current BMS HRT equivalents website page[3] which directs us that three sprays of Lenzetto is the equivalent of a 50mcg patch or two pumps of Oestrogel.

---

3. Taken from Women's Health Concern document for GPs and other health professionals. (Published March 2022)

Tablets

As with patches, the oral tablets are available as estrogen-only or combined. If you receive the combined hormones, which will be indicated by two different coloured tablets in your pack, you must take them in the right order, just as with the patches. The tablet form of combined HRT contains a body identical estrogen and a synthetic progesterone.

When moving to HRT tablets from another HRT format, the absorption is often more effective so it may be more appropriate to start on a lower dose than was previously given with patches, gel or spray. It is easier to adjust upwards if necessary.

There is a small increased blood clot risk with the tablets so anyone with a history of blood clots, ongoing migraines or who is very overweight, should opt for a transdermal option but can still take HRT.

Utrogestan and Prometrium progesterone tablets do not appear to pose this small blood clot risk so even though they are also tablets, the risk does not apply.

Bijuve tablets (also known as Bijuva)

This combined HRT tablet is a relatively new but lesser-known HRT star. It is the only HRT tablet that contains both body-identical estrogen and a body-identical progesterone. Early studies show it does not have the same blood clot risk as other HRT tablets.

The Mirena coil

The Mirena coil contains a synthetic progesterone called levonorgestrel, but only a very small amount of the hormone enters the bloodstream. As I mentioned earlier, this is classed as continuous progesterone and most women do not have a bleed when they have a Mirena coil fitted.

A little comment about progesterone-only HRT regimes:

It is relatively common for perimenopausal women to be told they don't need estrogen or should not take estrogen and are only prescribed progesterone such as the Mirena coil or the progesterone-only contraceptive pill to alleviate their symptoms.

There is some merit in progesterone being added in to alleviate some early symptoms such as erratic periods or anxiety but in essence, the symptoms of perimenopause and menopause are caused by low and fluctuating *estrogen*. Estrogen and progesterone are both hormones but they're not the same.

Offering you progesterone-only for perimenopausal symptoms management is like saying, *"I see you're deficient in apples. Here, let me give you an orange to help with that."*

PATIENCE AND PERSISTENCE

When you start HRT, please don't assume that if you don't feel amazing after a few months, the HRT is not working for you. You have many more options to try.

When deciding to start HRT, it's important to ensure you're happy with your choice and feel fully informed. There is no point in you taking something whilst feeling anxious about it or unhappy with your choice as this just sets you up for more anxiety and upset.

If you need more time to get yourself in the right headspace and become more fully informed then that's what you need.

CHAPTER SIX

EVERYTHING'S DRYING UP!

If ever I am in front of my TV when those well-known female incontinence pad adverts pop up, step away, as I will be shouting.

In many circles, it seems to be quite casually accepted and even expected that as women age or when they have had children, they will no longer be able to control their bladders and should expect to pee themselves when they laugh, sneeze, jump, run or just exist!

A client of mine recently said in an online comment:

"The look on Jane's face was priceless when I said that surely leaking when I laugh, or run was to be expected, but I have not had a problem since starting the simple topical treatment."

The adverts tell us how wonderful their pads are so we can 'let it all go'. They should be telling us that if this is a hormone related problem, there is an easy way to help sort it and there will be no more accidents or need for the pads.

I was shouting as I typed those words. I think I need to lie down.

I want to add that I totally accept there are times when bladder leak protection is necessary such as post-surgery, post-pregnancy, when HRT balance has not yet been achieved or of course when the problem is not hormone related, but women should be informed of **all** *the options available to them and not led to believe that incontinence is to be expected as we age.*

We have a lot of estrogen receptors in the bladder, vagina and vulva areas so the low and fluctuating hormone levels of peri and post-menopause can result in bladder and vaginal changes. The associated challenges are collectively referred to as Genitourinary Syndrome of Menopause (GSM), also known as atrophy, and can affect your vagina and bladder in quite impactful ways.

About eighty percent of menopausal women experience symptoms related to GSM but only around *eight* percent currently receive treatment!

YOUR BLADDER

Menopause related bladder issues are caused by the low estrogen in those important estrogen receptors at the neck of the bladder, making it very unhappy.

Low or fluctuating hormone levels can result in bladder changes which are caused by an overactivity of the estrogen receptors as they try to retain some balance. The impact of this can increase the regularity of needing to pee, bring about episodes of urine leakage and an urgency to pee, or even total urinary incontinence. Your poor bladder is just asking for help.

You may feel that you never quite empty your bladder or feel a sense of urgency to go with little warning or time to get to the toilet. This can have the knock-on effect of increasing anxiety or developing a 'toilet anxiety' which stops you from taking trips out unless you're near a toilet at all times.

This process can affect your sleep, as you may have to get up multiple times a night, which won't help your anxiety or mood, of course.

If there is pain or unexpected bleeding when going to the toilet, this needs to be checked by your doctor and a urine test is always a good idea with any changes, but if perimeno-pause or menopause is in the mix then hormones are a good place to start.

YOUR VAGINA AND VULVA

For clarity, just in case you need it: the vagina is the inside area of your female genitals, and the vulva is the outside area.

The impact of vaginal atrophy, which is essentially the skin drying up in the vagina and vulva areas (nice thought!), can extend into all areas of a woman's life, including what she can wear. Wearing trousers can be very uncomfortable and being able to, or even wanting to have sex, can be up for debate with the prospect of the discomfort to consider.

If you do experience this symptom, it is likely to worsen over time unless treated.

The vagina and the vulva are sensitive to lots of changes including hormones, medications, stress, food and much more, so it's important to know your own normal and to make sure you attend any gynaecological checks that you need to attend. That said, if you feel dryness, burning or itching and have skin that seems to be splitting in that area, it's worth considering the possibility of GSM.

I have a lot of older clients who have come to me after suffering immense pain and discomfort for decades with no idea why or what to do about it. The thinning of the skin in the vulva area can feel like a thousand paper cuts where the skin splits and tears because it is so fragile.

By the way! Let's not forget our little friend the clitoris. Some women report a decrease in sensitivity and almost disappearance of their little friend! Who knew that might happen? Panic not. The following treatments work on that area too.

For GSM there is a mild estrogen cream or pessary to gently replace the estrogen inside the vagina and at the neck of the bladder, although the cream is better on the vulva as you can apply it directly to the point of irritation. The treatment is very safe and can deal with symptoms such as bladder leakages, bladder irritation, itching, pain, splits, tears and burning in only a few weeks or even days. You can also use it as an ongoing treatment.

You may actually have thrush, or another infection so ask for a swab to check this when you ask for the estrogen treatment. However, don't accept that recurrent UTIs or thrush are just bad luck as low estrogen can make you more susceptible to them.

I remember after yet another thrush episode in my late thirties being told by a male doctor that, *"Women are just not meant to wear trousers."*

Once again, I'll just let that sit with you for a moment.

And back to the real world… Ask for the topical vaginal estrogen and see how you go whilst also requesting the swab.

In the following section, I have listed some examples of GSM treatments. They may not always be available as supplies and brands change all the time:

- Ovestin cream, also known as Ovestinon in some non-UK countries
- Vagifem pessaries
- Gina pessaries
- Estriol cream
- Estring, a rubbery type of ring inserted into the vagina and left in for three months
- Intrarosa, containing DHEA which converts to estrogen and androgens like testosterone
- Blissel, which is very low dose
- Estrace, mostly available in the USA

Not every woman will experience symptoms of GSM but if you do, you can fix the problem.

If you notice any white shiny patches on the vulva, this may be something called lichen sclerosis (LS) which is completely different. It needs steroid treatment at a separate time from any other treatment, so please address this with your doctor.

This is important to note:

Many women are told they cannot have vaginal estrogen alongside their systemic or main HRT in patches, gel, tablets, etc. This is totally untrue.

Vaginal estrogen is a topical treatment so only works on the area of application. It is low dose, safe and effective for women of any age, including women with a poor health history.

CHAPTER SEVEN

HYSTERECTOMY AND PROLAPSE

This chapter details my personal voyage to pelvic health after many years of trying to access help to fix my bowel prolapse. I have written it in a light-hearted way, but this is not to diminish the fact that hysterectomy and prolapse repair are major operations.

The main reason for sharing my story is primarily to help anyone who is experiencing signs and symptoms of prolapse or pelvic organ dysfunction, to remove the fear and confusion from the process of trying to work out what is happening.

You will see that I had my operation carried out vaginally so, unlike an abdominal hysterectomy, there was no incision on my stomach to worry about. In some cases, surgeons need to take a more traditional abdominal route. For example, you may have large fibroids which would make the vaginal route too difficult but either way, the result is the same.

THE BACKGROUND

You might assume that as I help women to take control of their gynaecological health, I have my own pelvic health totally on point and that I live a life of rainbows and kittens.

Not so.

I coach many women every week on how not to accept debilitating symptoms and how to speak confidently to their doctors to access what they need. However, from the age of about forty I had been putting up with the increasingly debilitating impact of a bowel prolapse, known as a rectocele. When I say, 'putting up with', it was more a case of not being able to access the right help.

The prolapse was probably initially caused by birthing my 11.5lb son but was likely made much worse by the low estrogen of perimenopause.

In Chapter Six, where I talk about genitourinary syndrome of menopause (GSM), I mention the thinning skin caused by low estrogen. You may be interested/horrified to know that this can also impact and degrade pelvic floor muscle strength, causing the bladder, bowel or uterus to prolapse.

This basically means that one or more of the pelvic organs has fallen down from its usual position as the supporting muscles have weakened, which is what happened to me. As we often do, I had adapted to the ever-increasing symptoms of this.

In 2022, aged fifty-five, I also had a very temperamental uterus which was annoying me on a regular basis with post-menopausal bleeding. I was becoming tired of having internal investigations, which fortunately all showed no serious problem.

Any unexpected or unscheduled bleeding needs to be checked by a doctor, of course, but I knew my uterus lining was fine, even though an ovarian cyst was identified on a few occasions which was apparently of no concern. I also seemed to be spending a large percentage of my time with extreme bloating and stomach problems, which I assumed were due to the prolapse.

If bloating and bowel problems are new symptoms for you, they always need checking out with your doctor. They are usually nothing to worry about but could be caused by other more serious problems such as bowel cancer. I had experienced some form of bowel upset for many years so didn't view these symptoms as new.

I had been asking for medical intervention for my prolapse for years but was made to feel I was making a fuss and that *'it's common'*, *'not a problem'* and *'nothing serious'*. Although I would not recommend waiting fifteen years to act, this was merely the point by which I had reached my limit and I paid to have the operation done privately.

Although not life-threatening, it was extremely life-impacting and limited my ability to enjoy life. At one stage I was supporting women with their hormones whilst unable to be far from a toilet due to my bowel problems.

By 2022, I would have paid anything to improve my situation. In the end, it was considerably less than I had expected, and you will see that it was the best decision I ever made.

But I'm jumping way too far ahead.

IN THE BEGINNING

I begin my tale when I was thirty-two and having my second child. Yes, the huge one who is now a perfectly proportioned 6'4" grown man.

My insides were treated less than lovingly. Who knew that giving birth to an 11.5lb baby would wreak havoc with my pelvic organs? I was not offered any aftercare or information, so I quite simply got on with life as I allowed the haemorrhoids to heal.

Fast forward five years or so to what I now know was the start of perimenopause, and it was becoming clear that things were not the same as they used to be.

Are My Insides Falling Out?

The simple answer to the above question was no, my insides were not falling out, but over time I became aware of some unwanted symptoms, aside from my other perimenopausal symptoms. My body had coped relatively well until perimenopause but then my pelvic muscles popped on their slippers and dressing gown, picked up a good book and sat down to chill.

When the pelvic floor muscles which support our pelvic organs weaken, this can often aggravate a previous weakness. You don't actually need to have a previous weakness, though. Even if you haven't had children you may still have a prolapse in the future so pelvic floor exercises and avoiding becoming constipated are key to sidestepping this.

I have been asked many times how you would know that you have a prolapse. It is different for everyone, but you may become aware of being more constipated and more bloated.

You may feel a dragging sensation when going to the toilet to poop. You may also be aware that you need to pee more often and can't easily empty your bladder, or the need to do so becomes an urgent need to poop as well.

This is due to the muscles which usually hold everything in their correct places having become too weak to do their job properly, resulting in lots of pushing and elbowing for space in your pelvis. If, like mine was, your prolapse is quite severe you may feel or see a bulge popping out of your vagina when you go to the toilet. You may have had to push on the posterior (back) vaginal wall to even get a poop to come out.

This is life-impacting and often means that when you need to go… you need to go! It is almost like the safety mechanism in your bottom has broken. The impact for me was years of extreme bowel upset and toilet anxiety.

It isn't life-threatening but it's very inconvenient and can feel quite scary and uncomfortable. The bulging can also protrude much more than it did in my own experience. It may be there all the time and make sitting down very uncomfortable.

What About the Uterus?

I didn't have a prolapsed uterus but when I finally made an appointment to see a specialist in London, my uterus was also in my line of sight. The specialist listened to me ramble on about bowel and toilet problems for, I expect, longer than he wanted to, and then he needed to have a look at the problem.

I feel he was slightly taken aback by my lack of embarrassment and the speed with which I leapt on that couch! When I sat back down, I felt quite emotional hearing him say,

"Yes, you have quite a severe bowel prolapse there." He actually believed me!

I was so happy and thanked him for not dismissing my concerns. This is exactly how many of my clients respond during my own consultations and is exactly why I do what I do.

Although I was clearly there to sort my prolapse, I was also keen to be rid of my uterus which had served her purpose in producing my lovely children but now needed to leave me in peace to enjoy my menopause. Being prone to prolapse, there was a good chance I would have a uterine prolapse following the surgery, so my new best friend and I agreed that a hysterectomy was appropriate.

I requested, or maybe I insisted, on a complete hysterectomy: therefore, my uterus, fallopian tubes, ovaries and cervix would all be removed together. As a post-menopausal woman, my ovaries had retired a long time ago and I had no desire to have my tubes and ovaries floating about in my pelvic area with no uterus. The cervix removal was just a bonus for me and meant no more cervical cancer concerns.

I had been having regular pelvic scans, biopsies and polyp removals since being post-menopausal which had always been clear and successful, but they were not pleasant, and each one was a drain on NHS resources.

Ultimately, at my age and with my plans to travel and get on with life, I was ready to part ways with it all.

ASKING QUESTIONS

Once I had made the decision to get everything sorted, I was on a mission. If this sounds like you, then you will make your own decisions based on your individual needs and wants. My experience is my experience, but you need to do what's right for you.

I came away from that appointment with a list of questions I was not yet ready to ask. It was important to take time to consider them. They included: Will sex be any different after the operation and how much shorter will my vagina be? You know, everyday questions like that.

During the consultation, I was clear about my desired end results, which were, a bowel that was not constantly trying to escape from my body and no temperamental uterus.

What to Ask

I bloody *love* a list so there were plenty of lists in my planning for the appointment, followed by a list of what I wanted to consider further, then a list of questions to ask at my follow-up telephone appointment.

Key questions and the Responses:

"I assume my bowel and bladder op will not involve any of the mesh that has caused so many problems?"

Definitely no mesh. We will cut a diamond-shaped section from the inside of the vagina and then stitch the sides together to improve the strength of bowel support. We will also assess the bladder and do the same on that side if required.

"I know I am here to discuss bowel surgery, but can you remove my uterus too, please?"

Errr... will I try to persuade you to have a hysterectomy? No.

Can you persuade me to perform a hysterectomy on you at this stage? Yes. You are likely to need one in ten to twenty years anyway and have had regular problems with post-menopausal bleeding, so it's sensible.

"Will I have my cervix removed?"

Yes.

"Can I also have my ovaries removed even though they are not a problem?"

We may not be able to reach them during the vaginal surgery, but we will try if that's what you want.

"How long is my recovery likely to be?"

Around six weeks but you will need to move regularly every day. No lifting of anything heavier than a loaf of bread early on.

OPERATION DAY

So, the day arrived and we had a three-hour drive to the hospital. Roger was used to having to stop at every toilet on the way to anywhere, so my nervous tummy was no surprise. The joys of bowel issues!

On arrival, I had bloods and blood pressure taken as part of my pre-op assessment. I had asked to have these done on the same day to avoid travelling twice but you are usually expected to visit the hospital a few days before your operation, so it's worth factoring this into your plans.

I was amused to be told I needed to take a pregnancy test. I totally understand the reasoning for asking this of many hysterectomy patients, but even when I told them I was a long time post-menopausal and had been sterilised in the 1990s, they told me it was still necessary. When I explained my situation more clearly to the nursing assistant, she was happy for me to sign a disclaimer instead.

If I had been pregnant it would have been a medical miracle based on the above, but I understand their caution.

There was a lot of waiting around so I told Roger to go and find something to do for a few hours which meant I could focus on the job in hand. I find it very calming to focus on the task in front of me.

Although I arrived at the hospital by ten am, I actually ended up having to wait until 5.30 pm for my operation. This was two hours later than planned so I was dehydrated by then, not having had anything to drink since seven that morning.

It is worth checking on timings as the day progresses. My anaesthetist told me just before I was put under anaesthetic that I could have had some water during the day, but as I then told him I was feeling dehydrated he very kindly upped my fluids during the operation to help me out.

Bearing in mind that this was a bowel prolapse repair as well as a hysterectomy, you will not be surprised to read that my bowel was running scared all that day! Bless it.

I probably pooped the majority of my innards out, but I consider this a very selfless service for my surgeon. He had not asked me to do any bowel 'prep' beforehand so me pooping on the operating table was a strong possibility.

What to Pack:

I packed way too much stuff, but I can recommend the following essentials.

- Nice pyjamas for when you're ready to get changed after surgery as they make you feel more human.
- A film or two on your iPad in case the TV is rubbish.
- Books were a waste of time for me as I couldn't concentrate, but you may enjoy a good book.
- Lip balm as surgery is very drying.
- Sanitary protection in case they don't provide enough for you.
- Water-only wet wipes for post-surgery hygiene. You may not feel like a shower.
- Loose clothes to return home in, especially if you have had an abdominal incision.
- Usual toiletries to make you smell and feel good.
- Some peppermint sweeties in case you feel windy as they will likely fill your abdomen with air during the op. I didn't need mine as I felt fine.
- I also used a relaxing sleep app of which there are lots if you search the app store. It was very reassuring when I didn't feel great and needed to take my mind off things.

THE OPERATION

About an hour before the op, I changed into my delicious hospital gown and paper knickers, which were only slightly better than being totally naked from the rear view, but even the sexy surgical stockings and slipper socks didn't dampen my joy.

Ask for help the first time you need to put on the ever-attractive surgical stockings. They are pretty tight for good reason, and it takes time to learn what process works for you, but they need to be on to help prevent blood clots post-surgery and for weeks afterwards, so you may as well make friends with them.

So… socks, paper pants and revealing gown on, and off we toddled to the operating area.

As I arrived, I said a fond 'Hi' to my surgeon and reminded him I needed a photo of all the removed gynae bits and bobs. *"It is an unusual request,"* he said, but he was happy to go along with it if only to shut me up.

In a small but very welcoming room, I had a chat with the anaesthetist whom I already knew as we had spoken and met a few times. I felt quite relaxed and happy to get going.

I asked the nursing team to please make sure I was given my glasses as soon as I woke up. Without them I am very limited in my ability to focus on anything. I also reminded the team to leave my HRT patches alone. I think they got the message as I was very persistent.

The anaesthetic lines were put into the back of my hand and the anaesthetist asked me what my favourite alcoholic drink was.

"Red wine," I replied.

"Ok then… this will feel like three red wines so enjoy."

He was right... and I did.

I was told to breathe deeply through the mask over my mouth and nose and the next thing I knew, I was waking up in recovery.

IN RECOVERY

If you've ever had a general anaesthetic, you will know how the waking-up process feels.

On waking, that initial second was a realisation of where I was, followed by a brief attempt to remove the tube from my throat. This was quickly removed by the nurse, and I was hardly aware of the process. It is important they leave the tube in until they are sure you are awake and no longer need breathing support.

My main memory of this particular experience was the odd smell. Not a hospital smell but still clinical, and the huge amount of activity around me with nurses and doctors all carrying out their role in my care. It was impressive!

I remember having my glasses put on even though my eyes were closed and the nurse very sweetly saying, *"What pretty glasses."*

It was important positivity when I needed it.

There was no pain and only slight nausea. I managed to look at the clock so could see that the operation had taken longer than expected, which told me that maybe things hadn't quite gone to plan.

BACK IN MY ROOM

Roger was in the room waiting for me and when I was wheeled in he thought I was still unconscious. I was aware of what was going on but was really sleepy. After a few minutes, he tells me that he saw a little hand peep over the top of the bed safety bars for him to hold.

I now know I had quite low blood pressure which was the main reason for the longer operation time. I know that being dehydrated also lowers blood pressure, but during that night, I kept falling asleep every time I went to have a drink, so I was pretty useless at managing that! but I was monitored and woken up to be checked on a regular basis.

When Roger left that night, I was hooked up to painkillers, fluid, a blood pressure machine, and a catheter so that I didn't need to get up for the toilet, and both legs had inflating cuffs on them to periodically squeeze my lower legs. These are like blood pressure cuffs and help stop blood clotting. I know many find these annoying, but I found them quite soothing.

I was still pretty groggy and not very impressed to have my evening meal placed in front of me one hour after my operation. I think if the timings of my operation had been as planned, I may have welcomed a hearty meal, but an hour after the op I was not up for a gourmet mix of fish and vegetables. Having said that, fluids were more important, so no major issue.

That night I was in a moderate amount of pain, but mostly just like a bad period pain. I had a lot of intravenous painkillers but was also in charge of a little button to top myself up every ten minutes if necessary. Luckily the machine stops you topping up too much or too often, otherwise, I feel I may have done myself some harm!

I asked about the pain and was told this was likely due to the large amount of vaginal packing in place to stem bleeding, in the same way as putting pressure on a cut. This would put pressure on the posterior wall stitches from the bowel repair and the top of the vagina where the cervix had been removed leaving me with a 'vault' where everything is sealed off.

Sounds so sexy and alluring, doesn't it?

As a result of all that, I had virtually no sleep that first night but felt ok and the pain was nagging but not bad.

The next morning, I was given more oral painkillers and breakfast which I forced down because I have always taken the approach that I will do everything I need to do to get better, and eating is one of those things, but I was *not* hungry!

In the weeks prior to the operation, I had been taking vitamin C and zinc, which are excellent for their healing properties. I continued taking them afterwards, stopping the zinc supplement three months after the operation.

Seventeen hours after my surgery, Roger came to see me, but my room was empty. He wondered whether he had missed a call to let him know I hadn't made it, but I was with the physiotherapist in my own clothes, walking along the corridor, not hooked up to any wires at all!

Even I was impressed that I could do that.

Vaginal Packing

I mentioned earlier that the pain I felt in my uterus area was very period-like and that the pressure of the packing was the cause, so it was a relief to be told that this was coming out at around eleven am the day after surgery.

It was quick to remove but, good lord, there was a lot of it! Who knew I had so much space inside there?

It was pretty low as far as pain levels go. The process was to breathe in just before the nurse started to extract it, which she did in stages, and to breathe out as she extracted. It was just a bit uncomfortable and felt very odd, but it went on *forever!*

I didn't ask for the measurement, but it felt like about twenty feet of gauze came out.

When it was out it was so much better; the pain stopped almost immediately.

Bleeding

Bleeding wasn't an issue for me, but this obviously varies. I had expected more with my surgery, but it was minimal.

Pooping

My next challenge was going to be pooping! After having the bowel prolapse repair, my bowel was very unhappy. I knew the team wouldn't let me leave until I had pooped so it was key to eat what I was given and to move about as much as possible.

I also tried to limit my oral painkillers at this stage as the ibuprofen was not helping with my bowel movement.

Although the clinical team were rightly concerned that I should have adequate pain relief to ensure my blood pressure remained stable and I felt well, I needed to have a good balance, which for me, did not include so many painkillers.

I was peeing perfectly fine and actually felt amazing. My main challenge at this stage was definitely the pooping!

Beware post-surgery euphoria which can make you think all is well and you don't need to rest. *You do!*

So… now my bowel had to comply, so this was a battle of wills. It was important to drink lots of water, eat lots of fibre and not to strain, particularly with those stitches to consider. In the end, the team gave me Movicol, a type of laxative. This made me feel sick. I prefer senna products and they worked well but it's a slow process and a lot was mindset oriented after years of bowel upset. We got there in the end, and I was released to go home.

Just prior to going home after three days, I spoke with my surgeon who mentioned my ovarian 'cyst' being large and having to send it to pathology.

That was unexpected.

HOME AGAIN

I am terrible at sitting still unless I'm asleep, and even then I'm not very still, but an anaesthetic takes that decision out of your hands.

I was totally wiped out for a few days and the pooping worries took many weeks to settle. I needed to start to trust my body again after it had misbehaved for so long. There were good and bad days and walking or pottering about was essential to help my bowel and to avoid blood clots, but I was back working with clients after seven days as my role mostly involves me listening and talking so is not physically challenging.

My HRT regime changed to estrogen-only from the day of my surgery as no uterus meant no need for progesterone in my case. I don't feel I benefit from it in any other way.

Over the following four to five months, I realised I needed to increase my dose of estrogen to rediscover my hormone balance, which my doctor was fine with after we went through the details of my returning symptoms.

I would always advise that you allow your body a few months to settle post-surgery or illness before making HRT changes. You may not need a change. Your body may just need more time.

OVARIAN SURPRISE

That title makes it sound like a fun summer pudding. It wasn't.

You'll remember that I insisted my ovaries were removed. This wasn't because I had some sort of premonition, but let's say I'm glad I'm so feisty!

My surgeon sent the ovary off for testing and it seems that my 'cyst' was actually a slow-growing ovarian strumal carcinoid: a cancerous ovarian tumour. I definitely didn't order that!

It is very rare. Only 0.3-1 percent of all ovarian tumours are like this. My surgeon is a gynaecology cancer expert and he had only seen one in his whole career. I like to be part of the elite crowd but maybe not this one. As it is so rare, the treatment and ongoing monitoring is a bit of an unknown, so everyone was running a bit blind with it all.

I have since learnt a lot about these incognito tumours, including the fact that they produce adrenaline which explained the unexpected rushes of anxiety I sometimes felt when relaxing. Additionally, it seems that most of my increased bloating and extreme gut upset were caused by my alien friend, as since the operation, I have had almost no gut issues at all.

For now, I am seen by the specialist every six months or so to be injected with radioactive liquid and sent for a PET CT scan to check that the tumour has not returned somewhere else in my body. I will be having these tests for five years and then considered to be clear.

I am grateful that I work in women's health as this gave me the knowledge and confidence to ask for what I needed at a crucial time in my own health. I hope that my experience helps others to do the same but, just to reiterate: My tumour was rare, and most cysts are just that – ordinary cysts with no connection to tumours so there is no need to worry that your cyst is anything sinister. However, any odd changes need to be checked by your doctor.

There are so many reasons for deciding to have a hysterec-tomy, some much more serious than others. I hope you feel that if it's on the cards for you, you can embrace the oppor-tunity to feel better than you do. Nobody wants to have an operation but if it's what you need and it will help your longer-term health, you know what to do.

PELVIC FLOOR

Just a little extra info about our lovely and often neglected pelvic floor.

Pooping is important from a pelvic floor perspective. When you become constipated this can impact your pelvic floor and not in a good way. It can further stress those pelvic muscles and result in both an urgency to pee and potential for a bowel prolapse. The good news is that you can do something about that.

You may be constipated due to stress, nutrition or sitting down too much. In my case, I was often constipated due to my prolapsed bowel which then became a stress all of its own. If you are not able to relax, you can't poop well.

Am I a little obsessed with pooping? Maybe.

What to Do?

Some gentle abdominal massage, regular movement, drinking plenty of water each day and making sure you incorporate fibre into your diet which can be as simple as whole vegetables and fruit.

Some find that using a squatty potty is useful, but this will depend on any prolapse and the angle of that.

As I mention in Chapter Eleven, I highly recommend making sure you *relax* and take *time* to visit the toilet. Dashing in and out is not giving your body the chance to do what it must do, and you are less likely to fully or even partly complete the task.

POST-OP HEALTH

As I write these words it is over eighteen months since my operation. I can happily report that I no longer have the bowel challenges of the previous ten to fifteen years but am aware that I must nurture my pelvic floor to avoid a repeat prolapse. With my erratic brain, remembering to do my pelvic floor exercises is a challenge.

As far as the hysterectomy is concerned, I have not noticed any ill effects or changes other than never needing to think about my post-menopausal bleeding ever again so *yay* for that. Clearly, I am not recommending a major operation unless you need it, but hopefully you feel reassured that if you do need it, you can embrace the process.

Questioning Is Key

I am a to-the-point, no-nonsense kind of person but I know that not everyone finds it easy to talk about personal topics. Honesty and clarity will help you to achieve your health goals.

I asked very blunt questions of my specialists, and my willingness to talk about these seemingly embarrassing issues has resulted in me overcoming my health problems. It is much better to risk a moment of awkwardness than to put up with feeling awful. It does become easier the more you do it too.

I say the word vagina almost every day now but maybe that's a step too far for most.

CHAPTER EIGHT

PROGESTERONE, PMDD & HISTAMINE INTOLERANCE

The chapter title seems like a lot, but these three can overlap with each other so it's sensible to look at them together.

Premenstrual dysphoric disorder (PMDD) is like premenstrual syndrome (PMS) but much more serious. It is also like a progesterone intolerance but a more severe version of this. Many women with PMDD appear to be sensitive to the fluctuations in hormone levels which do not affect others. It is thought that PMDD affects about one in twenty women.

It can cause a wide range of symptoms a week or two before your period. However, please don't assume you have PMDD if you have some version of the symptoms listed a little further on. This is likely not to be the case.

Many of the symptoms are perimenopausal-type symptoms but PMDD can hugely accentuate these during the high progesterone weeks. Balance is key to hormone happiness and never more so than in the case of PMDD.

Access Support

If you feel you are experiencing PMDD, you can find more information and resources at the mind.org.uk website.

You can find more information on histamine intolerance at histamineintolerance.org.uk and Dr Tina Peers is a highly regarded specialist in this area. You can find her on drtinapeers.com.

Monitor how you feel and the severity of your symptoms during the month and speak to your doctor or a PMDD specialist if you feel that this applies to you.

PROGESTERONE

I have a few clients with PMDD, and it is really important in such cases to spend time listening to their experiences and the impact of such. Many have already been dismissed, belittled or just not taken seriously regarding their symptoms for years, which has often all but ruined their lives up to that point.

PMDD can cause severe depression or anxiety in the week or two before your period starts and can lead to some women feeling unable to cope. Symptoms usually go away two to three days after a period starts but the impact of the disruption is left behind.

You may have a sensitivity or slight intolerance to certain body identical progesterones or synthetic progesterones, but this is not as common as it seems, so there's no need to feel anxious about starting HRT.

Progesterone is vital to protect the uterus lining when we introduce estrogen and in most cases it is a relaxant and can have a calming effect on our bodies, but in some cases, it can cause a feeling of anxiety, with a number of women experiencing this more extreme sensitivity.

You may be one of those who enjoy the higher progesterone element of your cycle. You will know this as you feel calmer and more balanced when you are not on your period, which is when your natural progesterone levels are higher. If you're on HRT, these are the weeks when you are taking the progesterone element of the regime.

During this time the progesterone converts to a neurosteroid which calms GABA receptors. You may have heard of or been given a drug called gabapentin which does the same. This then acts as a sedative. High progesterone (during pregnancy for example) can make you feel sleepy. The synthetic progesterone in birth control pills does not convert in this way so doesn't offer this benefit.

If a woman suffers with PMDD, her body does not convert the progesterone to a neurosteroid, and she will not feel the same effect. She may instead feel anxious, angry or depressed. Some feel suicidal and hopeless.

If you are feeling very low and hopeless, please seek professional help from your doctor. If you feel in need of urgent help, you can contact SHOUT at giveusashout.org or The Samaritans at samaritans.org for confidential support.

Some Known Emotional Symptoms of PMDD

- Mood swings
- Feeling upset or tearful
- Lack of energy
- Less interest in activities you normally enjoy
- Feeling hopeless
- Suicidal feelings
- Feeling angry or irritable
- Feeling anxious
- Feeling tense or on edge
- Feeling overwhelmed or out of control
- Difficulty concentrating

Some Physical and Behavioural Symptoms of PMDD

- Breast tenderness or swelling
- Pain in your muscles and joints
- Headaches
- Feeling bloated
- Changes in your appetite, such as overeating or having specific food cravings
- Sleep problems
- Increased anger or conflict with people around you
- Becoming very upset if you feel that others are rejecting you

Symptoms list taken from mind.org.uk (May 2024)

What Can You Do?

Selective serotonin reuptake inhibitors (SSRI) are a commonly used type of antidepressant which have historically been used for PMDD. It is also sometimes useful to calm those fluctuations with the birth control pill. However, some SSRI drugs can increase the risks of osteoporosis, and birth control can cause mood and libido issues, so caution is required for longer-term use.

Stopping Hormone Production

Our hormones help us manage our long-term health, so stopping our hormones long-term is not ideal, especially when we are looking to add in hormones to support peri and post-menopause. Having said that, it is sometimes necessary for the short term and wellbeing of the PMDD sufferer.

From an HRT perspective, we try to find the right balance between estrogen and progesterone so that a woman with PMDD can benefit from her HRT but also have a safe and manageable dose of progesterone. This may be a lower dose of progesterone or a progesterone dose that is only administered quarterly. In such cases, this needs to be monitored by a doctor.

Some women with extremely life-impacting symptoms will be advised to have a hysterectomy to bypass the need to use progesterone as part of HRT, but this is not a first option. However, don't be frightened to ask about this option as it can be a positive step.

NON-MEDICAL HELP

There are several effective things you can do to help yourself if PMDD is your challenge.

Reducing Histamine

Histamine is important in our body's functions such as regulating the sleep-wake cycle and in managing cognitive function.

It also regulates many key bodily functions and processes such as the secretion of gastric acid, but when we have an overreaction to something this can make us feel ill in a variety of areas including the brain, skin, lungs and digestive system.

When taking HRT, a histamine intolerance (HIT) will usually become clear as soon as you start introducing estrogen to your system. It will manifest itself a bit like an allergy and you may feel really poorly with symptoms that include:

- Headaches or migraines
- Nasal congestion or sinus issues
- Fatigue
- Hives
- Digestive issues
- Irregular menstrual cycle
- Nausea
- Vomiting

I know from my own experiences that overproduction of histamine can generally make me feel quite inflamed and allergic. Too much wine, for example, makes me feel quite nasal with a stuffed-up head and too much dairy makes me itchy.

It has implications for our hormonal health and how we respond to the menopause and HRT, so it is an important area for further research and study.

I see a lot of women who assume they have a histamine intolerance as they start to feel worse again after a few weeks or months on HRT, but this is usually not the case. In most cases, an HRT dose adjustment is all that is needed.

HIT is not very common, but it is very poorly understood or acknowledged by the medical profession and often requires specialist help.

As a qualified nutritionist, I am all about addressing nutrition in addition to hormones, so you'll find some helpful guidance in Chapter Eleven but specifically with histamine in mind, you will find some really useful tips on histamineintolerance. org.uk including the following nutrition suggestions which are adapted from:

https://www.histamineintolerance.org.uk/about/the-food-diary/the-food-list/

HIT Nutrition

Avoid or reduce eating canned foods and ready meals.

Avoid or reduce eating ripened and fermented foods including older cheeses, alcoholic drinks, products containing yeast, and stale fish, as histamine levels in foods vary depending on their ripeness, maturity and hygiene.

- As much as possible, only buy and eat fresh products. Freshly cooked meals really help your body to prepare for eating.
- Don't allow foods to linger outside the refrigerator, especially meat products.

Lower Histamine Level Foods
(Good options with an intolerance)

- Fresh meat (cooled, frozen or fresh)
- Certain fish such as hake, trout and plaice
- Chicken
- Egg
- Fresh fruits with the exception of plantains
- Fresh vegetables with the exception of tomatoes, aubergine (aka eggplant) and spinach
- Grains including rice noodles, white bread, rye bread, rice crisp bread, oats, puffed rice crackers, millet flour and pasta
- Fresh pasteurised milk and milk products
- Goat and sheep milk
- Cream cheese, mozzarella, butter
- Most cooking oils
- Most leafy herbs
- Most fruit juices without citrus fruits

Higher Histamine Level Foods
(Aim to avoid with an intolerance)

- Alcohol
- Aubergine (aka eggplant)
- Tomatoes
- Spinach
- Pickled or canned foods
- Matured cheeses
- Smoked meat products: salami, ham, sausages
- Shellfish
- Beans and pulses: chickpeas, soy flour
- Long-stored nuts: peanuts, cashew nuts, almonds, pistachio
- Chocolates and other cocoa-based products
- Rice vinegar
- Ready meals
- Salty snacks, sweets with preservatives and artificial colourings

Supplements

I always recommend daily magnesium supplementation as, amongst other benefits, magnesium helps with the GABA response. 3-400mg of magnesium glycinate is good. If this upsets your tummy then reduce the dose, but this form of magnesium is usually gentle on tums.

It is good to add in **omega 3**, **vitamins B6, B12 and Taurine** (Taurine is usually calming and is available from good health food shops).

Whatever you decide, it's important to view the process as a search to find your perfect balance to achieve both short and long-term health and not to view your hormones as the enemy.

I recently asked one of my valued VIP members to put into words how her own PMDD affects her. This is what she had to say:

"It's like looking at yourself through a window, unable to control the actions and thoughts and having to wait for it to pass. Totally immobilising."

— **Rachel Fossett, May 2024**

CHAPTER NINE

TESTOSTERONE IN WOMEN: WHAT'S THE POINT?

Not really into the whole sex thing these days?

I hear a lot of experiences of low libido. It can take an enormous effort to discuss your most intimate challenges with a health professional and it can really hurt to be sent away with a feeling of not being heard, or of shame.

You may have heard some of these if you've told your doctor that you don't feel like having sex. These are actual responses received by a few of my clients during the past ten years.

"Just have a glass of wine and you'll be fine."

"Your husband needs you to get past that."

"Most women feel that way... it's normal at your age."

"If it hurts just use lots of lube."

None of the above responses are acceptable, valid or even humane.

Your lowered estrogen and/or testosterone levels can lead to you feeling this way as you lose your libido and feel sore and dry in your most intimate area.

IT'S NOT FOR GIRLS!

Remember that chocolate bar advert from the 1970s with the tagline *'It's not for girls!'*

This came to mind when one of my clients, desperate for help, was told by her doctor, *"Testosterone is a male hormone. It's not for women."*

Reminder fun fact!... Prior to perimenopause, women produce three to four times more testosterone than estrogen.

Some women cope well when their testosterone declines whereas others really struggle with sore joints, low libido and low mood. I have very sore hands when my levels are low.

Women often really have to fight even to be believed regarding symptoms. I have heard way too many reasons for not prescribing testosterone supplementation.

"You don't need a libido; you're over fifty so why would you?"

"You'll be more at risk of heart failure"

"You'll grow a beard and have a deeper voice."

In February 2023 there was a hugely biased article in a national newspaper filled with scaremongering about testosterone, including the risk of an enlarged clitoris, which is totally not based on fact when using the correct female dose. It is like saying, *"All fruit gives you diarrhoea,"* when in fact that is only likely to happen if you have too much of it.

Testosterone is produced in the ovaries and adrenal glands and it's important for bone preservation, energy levels and, of course, libido.

Symptoms of low testosterone levels:

- Low self-worth
- Low mood
- Low motivation
- Low libido
- Low pleasure levels

Potentially, it leads to:

- Bone loss
- Decreased muscle strength
- Memory changes

These symptoms may be due to low estrogen levels, so the usual practice is for your doctor to make sure your estrogen levels all look good before addressing the testosterone, but it's still very challenging to find support for low testosterone levels in women.

In the UK you're likely to need to visit a private doctor to access the female testosterone cream called Androfeme. It is imported from Australia and is quite an expensive option, so it is helpful if your GP is prepared to prescribe a testosterone gel for you.

The testosterone products currently available via your doctor are only licensed for men but are perfectly acceptable for female use as the dose can be altered to suit female needs. Women usually need one-tenth of the male dose.

The most popular options available via a GP in the UK are Testogel and Tostran.

If you access testosterone somewhere other than your GP, please ensure you only purchase your hormone replacement from a verified and reputable source such as a well-established online pharmacy or a private specialist doctor. There are many less than reputable sources for such things, so stick with your GP or private specialist who will also offer the appropriate dose and regime guidance.

Nobody has ever said that testosterone is a wonder drug, quick fix or magic and it isn't appropriate for every woman. It can take a few months to start to take effect, but I can confirm that many women find that testosterone is the missing piece of the hormone puzzle for them, and some cannot function well without it.

EVIDENCE

It is true that there is little clinical evidence of effective testosterone supplementation in women… but guess what? Historically, female sexual function, female pleasure and female hormone needs have been mostly ignored and dismissed so it's no surprise that the studies have not been carried out.

Although testosterone gels and creams are available for use by women, we need to work out and apply the correct amount to our skin, and as mentioned, use products originally designed for men. There is currently no approved testosterone delivery patch, which, like the estrogen and combined patches, would stick to the skin to easily deliver the hormone and likely only need changing once or twice a week.

However, in 2023 the world's first clinical trials of a new testosterone patch were announced. Researchers believe this move could transform lives globally: assuming anyone will actually prescribe it for women.

Dr Haitham Hamoda, the clinical lead for the menopause service at King's College Hospital and past chair of the British Menopause Society, said he welcomed the "*important*" development because if the trials were successful they "*will offer women more choice*".

Medherant, a company founded by the University of Warwick's Professor David Haddleton, started clinical trials examining the effect of the patch on libido in the autumn of 2023. Fingers crossed for future treatment.

If testosterone isn't for you and your libido is still pants, maybe the following will help.

Vitamin D and zinc supplements. Get your vitamin D and zinc checked by your doctor.

600mg a day of fenugreek has been shown to significantly improve sexual desire and energy levels.

Ginger has been shown to have a positive effect on sex drive.

As with any changes, try one thing at a time to see whether it works before moving on to another option.

Chapter Ten

SUPPORT FROM LOVED ONES

Menopause also affects the lives of husbands, partners and family members. No surprise there. It benefits everyone when we all work together towards the same goal. Even my own husband had to get with the programme. I was not an easy person to live with when perimenopausal and before starting HRT!

I have added this short chapter primarily to highlight how easy it can be for others to show empathy and understanding and to let my husband have his say.

Prior to starting HRT, I was told I was depressed and that my relationship must be at fault when my symptoms were overwhelming and impacting my ability to cope with life.

I wasn't and it wasn't.

I remember my mum having a pretty rough time of it when she was around forty-two years old. Of course, none of us knew what was wrong and she dealt with a lot of her symptoms by drinking too much alcohol and working too hard. Looking back at how she behaved when I was being a thirteen-year-old brat, she was most definitely struggling with low mood, anxiety and much more. Imagine the hormone hell of being perimenopausal whilst your daughter is pubescent! I expect many of you have experienced, or are experiencing this.

It is a challenge when neither you nor your partner knows what's going on. Far too many relationships break down solely due to the impact of menopause. The personality and health changes during perimenopause often happen so gradually that you're not even aware of them until communications between you have degenerated to such a level that there's a huge mountain to climb to get back on track.

Communicating to your loved one(s) how your perimenopausal symptoms make you feel can be challenging at best, but it's worth mentioning to them that you want things to improve just as much as they do. Nobody wants to feel rubbish or behave irrationally.

Having spoken with numerous husbands, partners and family members regarding frustrations about their relationships with women who are quite clearly peri or post-menopausal, I have outlined a few key summary points for you to share.

KEY SHARING POINTS

Perimenopause is the time leading up to full menopause and can last up to twelve years as the hormone levels begin to fluctuate and fall.

Menopause is the point in time when a woman has not had a period for twelve consecutive months.

Women have estrogen receptors attached to pretty much all their cells so this reduction in estrogen very often causes a wide range of symptoms, such as low mood, fatigue or low sex drive.

It's not just women over fifty who experience menopausal symptoms. Perimenopause and menopause can occur at any age after puberty although it is more common after aged forty-five.

Symptoms at forty to forty-five years are considered an early menopause, but it can start much earlier too and radical gynaecological surgery can throw a woman into menopause overnight! This is called a surgical menopause and can be challenging, often needing specialist medical advice to ensure a woman can continue to function as normal and stay healthy for the long term.

Some health changes such as IVF treatment, pregnancy, illness or certain medications can also bring on perimenopausal symptoms.

Many people, including medics, don't realise or accept that women also benefit from testosterone. We actually produce three to four times more testosterone than estrogen prior to perimenopause so it's a big player in the hormone party.

Although testosterone levels don't dip as quickly as estrogen levels, it's quite common for them to be significantly reduced during perimenopause. This important hormone can help to retain energy levels, boost brain clarity and keep that all-important sex drive active.

COMMON ISSUES RAISED BY HUSBANDS AND PARTNERS

"She's totally gone off sex!"

You may have a lack of interest in sex but not a lack of interest in your partner! Many of my clients tell me that they want to *want* sex. The lack of estrogen and testosterone means that the desire is missing. It feels like a part of them has just gone.

Part of the problem is also the physical pain or discomfort because of vaginal dryness and skin irritation which I cover in the chapter on genitourinary syndrome of menopause. Many women experience this dry, sore feeling both inside the vagina and on the vulva area, which is not a great mood enhancer. Imagine having to wear pants made of sandpaper every day with that scratchy, itchy, irritated feeling. No thanks.

"She's always exhausted."

The level of fatigue can be debilitating, especially if you are used to being energetic and busy and it brings about a unique tiredness that can stop you in your tracks, often leading to low mood caused by not being able to do what you love.

"Her mood is erratic. I never know what to say for the best."

During perimenopause, your mood may be changeable. Hormones fluctuate all the time so one day you will feel relatively ok, followed by a day of distress and the unknown. The fluctuating hormones can also cause or increase anxiety and bring about a very erratic mood which is totally out of your control. It can feel like a scary time but will also impact your relationships. Many women say they feel as if they're losing their minds.

"I'm worried that she drinks too much alcohol now."

Alcohol has an estrogenic effect so when the estrogen is depleted, the extra glass (or ten!) temporarily relieves the worst of the symptoms. You may not even realise this is why you crave booze. It just happens and then a pattern of coping behaviour is set.

HOW CAN YOUR LOVED ONE HELP?

The following words may help others to help you.

- Most peri and post-menopausal women say they struggle to explain how they feel, so being patient and asking you to try to put it into words will go a long way towards improving communication. I am a huge fan of talking things through… or maybe I'm just a huge fan of talking! I remember being quite surprised that my parents split up as they never seemed to argue, which clearly was part of the problem. Many years later, my youngest child looked very worried after Roger and I had been 'discussing' something in a fairly animated way. Some may call it arguing. My son said he was worried we would split up as we couldn't agree. I reassured him that this was normal behaviour and that people need to discuss things to understand each other better. Even when it feels uncomfortable or upsetting; it's necessary, to avoid negative feelings growing into resentment and then even worse, developing into apathy.

- Your loved one accompanying you to a specialist menopause appointment without passing judgment, is a great step. This will make you feel understood and supported, but also allow them to ask questions at the appointment and come away more informed.

- Your loved one becoming informed about your symptoms and the options available to you, shows a real commitment to helping. This could include HRT, nutrition and lifestyle changes.

- Most importantly, they should **try not to treat you as if you are less than you were** or are behaving irrationally. You may be feeling very unhappy with your symptoms and likely want to get things back to normal just as much as they do.

SOME WORDS FROM MR *MENOPAUSAL NOT MAD*®

"When Jane and I first met she was thirty-three. To my knowledge, she wasn't perimenopausal, but she was quick to tell me that she had been sterilised after her second child and was unable to have more children. Due to work and two families becoming one, we led a pretty stressful life for several years, so in some ways, this probably masked her early perimenopause symptoms, which we now know began around four years later.

I had no idea there was a problem other than Jane's quite erratic periods and any arguments were just disregarded in my mind as normal couple-type behaviour. I tend to be more future-focused, so I don't remember many of the occasions to which she refers, such as her throwing a chair at me in a fit of rage. I seem to have blocked that one out! but over the years Jane began to experience lower moods and a wide range of symptoms such as headaches and tiredness and generally, I wondered why she never seemed to be as healthy as she had been.

I am a solution-finder, so it was often frustrating for me not to be able to just fix the problem when she was feeling low or ill. It took a long time for me to really understand what was going on and this was only possible after Jane started to research everything for herself and share her knowledge with me. The rest, as they say, is history.

Nowadays when I meet other men around my age and mention what my wife does for a living, I am not necessarily surprised at how little they know about menopausal issues. However, when I meet women who are anywhere around perimenopausal age or older, I am constantly amazed at how little they know about this topic. The world would be a much better place if women were taught more about their bodies and men were informed about how women's bodies work. It would help their understanding as individuals, but importantly also as couples."

— **Roger Pangbourne (AKA Mr *Menopausal Not Mad*)**

CHAPTER ELEVEN

LOVE YOUR GUT

You may not know that as well as my menopause and HRT passion, I've been studying nutrition on and off since I was eighteen years old. I think we all know that this was not yesterday... but nearly forty years ago!

The gut health fads and advice change all the time, so I prefer to stick with logic and experience topped up with current data. Menopause is sometimes a challenge and HRT is great to get that hormonal balance right, but nutrition is important too. Your gut has its own brain you know, and it will thank you for your efforts.

Within this chapter, you'll learn some fundamental nutrition concepts to give you a solid grounding in the best way to nourish your body and support your gut. You'll find simple ways to begin moving your nutrition in the right direction to help your gut to help you.

To start you off, here are a few important tips.

- There are no teeth in your stomach so chew your food well. Aim for at least twelve chews per bite, which sounds a lot but it's more about not rushing your meals.

- Some foods help the gut to produce more good bacteria including garlic, onions, leeks, soaked oats, cooked rice and green bananas.
- Ginger, fennel and slippery elm are also fab.
- Boring I know, but limit your refined carbs, sugar, alcohol and processed food.

ESTROGEN AND THE GUT

You may be feeling bloated or 'blocked up'. This could be due to low estrogen.

One of the areas often impacted by lower estrogen levels is your gut, which affects many of your bodily functions, including your digestion.

Although I'm a huge advocate of HRT, I also know that some women choose not to take it and a very small percentage are unable to take it, so it's important to do everything possible to stay strong and healthy. Even if you do take HRT, it's still sensible to eat the right foods to help your gut to do its best for you.

It is kind of obvious that what you put into your body is going to affect your health and feelings of wellbeing during your peri and post-menopausal years, but it's even more important to try to take in food and drink that not only tastes good and gives you energy but empowers your body to fend off disease and heal quickly if you do become ill.

When you eat foods that harm or take in drinks that don't offer effective hydration, you're likely to experience increased susceptibility to disease and infection... plus the dreaded fatigue, brain fog, aches, pains and dehydrated skin associated with perimenopause.

The link between gut health and overall health is becoming much more well known, and during menopause your gut is already compromised from the reduced estrogen, so, you really need to get a handle on how to treat it well to help protect yourself from illness.

Some symptoms are aggravated by a poorly functioning gut so, if you suffer from anything like fibromyalgia or genitourinary symptoms, it's even more important to stay gut healthy.

Some foods are high in sugar or caffeine so although they provide a quick fix when you're tired or lacking in get up and go, you're very likely to have an energy crash soon afterwards.

Coffee is a firm favourite of many, but a cup of coffee will give you a boost and then make you feel tired thirty to sixty minutes later until you have another one. If you add sugar to your drink or eat biscuits with your cuppa, this will make the energy crash even worse.

It seems strange that a drink can dehydrate you but that's exactly what the caffeine does, including the caffeine in tea and energy drinks, which can result in headaches and fatigue which are already common symptoms of perimenopause.

Also, if you don't poop regularly your bowel is hoarding all sorts of toxins inside you, so a regular poop regime is a good thing. At least once a day, but two to three times a day is great.

Not pooping regularly?

Try regular sips of water throughout your day and it will add up, rather than the sometimes overwhelming six to eight glasses a day we are told we need, as this can seem a lot.

If you have trouble remembering to drink enough water, try creating prompts, like having a glass when you wake up or when you make a phone call. You could also add a reminder on your phone. It sounds a bit basic but you're trying to create a new habit. If the taste of plain water doesn't appeal to you, liven it up by infusing it with fresh sage which is also great to manage hot flushes or add a few crushed cranberries.

Make sure you move every hour and are not chained to your computer.

If things still get a bit stuck then apricots and prunes are great options to gently get it all moving again.

Don't forget to relax too. If you rush around like a stressy thing from stressy land then your bowel will not approve and is unlikely to behave.

Give yourself time to poop. None of this in and out in two minutes nonsense... but don't settle in for a few hours of phone scrolling either.

Soy

You may have heard that soy is a good thing for peri and post-menopause and that's true but be mindful that there is conflicting data on the benefits of individual isoflavones found in soy. For this reason, supplements containing high dose individual soy isoflavones are not as good as eating whole soy-based foods such as tofu, sushi, soya flour, soya milk and miso.

WHAT DOES YOUR GUT DO FOR YOU?

Your gut is your hero, actually! It has your back even when you abuse it with sugar, alcohol and toxins. It is your key defence against nasties and can help prevent you from becoming poorly and reduce the severity of an illness.

Let's take a short moment to appreciate your gut.

Weight

I don't get too involved in weight discussions as I am more focused on overall health management, but some studies have shown that being overweight can result in an altered gut microbiome, so it seems a logical move to try to change it back.

Women are often concerned about their weight in later life, but the important factor is not how you look, rather, how your body is able to cope and keep you well. There are many changes you can make to improve your gut health and enabling it to become effective at digesting and using the fuel from food is one of them.

If you eat the right foods, they will help you to feel fuller and more satisfied so you're less likely to snack but it's not one-size-fits-all with weight management, particularly during peri and post menopause. It may take a bit of back and forth to get your own blend of the right foods, hormone balance and exercise.

Live Bacteria

In this modern world of fast food and other less than natural ways to access nutrition, we often have a very low number of the right assorted bacteria in our gut.

The use of antibiotics has accentuated this as they kill off the good bacteria as well as the bad, which is why you often get thrush whenever you take a course of antibiotics. To remedy this, we may need to add in a live bacteria supplement. After illness I always try to do this to feed and nurture the good bacteria which may have been lost due to sickness or diarrhoea.

It is good practice to add in a daily live bacteria at a low dose to combat the less than healthy foods we all consume now and again. When you eat the less than gut friendly foods, you're inviting unfriendly bacteria into your system and allowing them to thrive. The live bacteria will boost the good stuff and help to keep your gut happy. The gut bacteria will have a chat with your brain, and the brain responds, obviously in its own neurotransmitter type of way. This then affects your moods, including your levels of happiness, pleasure and ability to be positive. If your gut is out of balance you're likely to feel grumpy, angry and tearful, which are also perimenopausal symptoms so it's important to straighten out your gut to give those hormones the best chance to work.

Even HRT can't fix a damaged gut!

Let's be honest with ourselves here. When we eat as if we don't care about the consequences, we're going to feel rubbish! I sometimes do it too so I'm not judging. Your poor gut microbiome can become so upset that you end up with an infection which brings inflammation, resulting in similar symptoms to perimenopause such as fatigue, low energy and weight gain.

Of course, this could be hormonal as well, but that upset gut can massively hamper your ability to feel better and for any HRT or lifestyle changes to work most effectively.

For the next seven days make a note of EVERYTHING you eat and drink and at the end of each day note how you feel. Tired, hyper, bloated, sore? This should help you to work out what helps and what hinders your own health.

KEEPING IT SIMPLE

Keeping up with what you're supposed to eat can seem complicated but there are only six key categories of essential nutrients to consider, so let me help you with that.

Essential nutrients are the substances you need from food because your body can't produce enough of them on its own. If you want to simplify healthy eating, focus on the six basics which are:

- Proteins
- Carbohydrates
- Fats
- Vitamins
- Minerals
- Water

All your calories come from the three **macronutrients,** which are protein, carbohydrates, and fats. These give you energy and you need them in large quantities.

In case you like the detail, I can tell you that the current dietary guidelines recommend you have:

45-65% of your total daily calories from carbohydrates

20-35% from fat

and

10-35% from protein.

What is Protein?

Protein is the major building block for your body's cells and tissues. It helps you increase muscle mass and boosts your metabolism. Good sources include fish, eggs, beans and dairy products.

What are Carbohydrates?

These are made up mostly of sugar, starch and fibre and are your main sources of energy. And no, that doesn't mean you can live on biscuits!

Refined sugars are classed as simple carbohydrates and give you that burst of energy like a sports drink or a packet of sweets; don't forget the crash after a sugar burst.

Starches need to break down in the body, so they release their energy much more slowly. Pasta would be a good example.

Although fibre doesn't provide energy in the usual way, it does good stuff by feeding the friendly bacteria in the gut. These bacteria then use the fibre to produce useful fatty acids that can be used as energy.

Fat Isn't the Enemy

Fat actually helps your body to store vitamins and to build up your cell membranes.

How do you access that good fat?

Well… it's in meat and dairy but also in healthy vegetables, nuts and seeds. If you choose the best fats for your body, you won't put on weight.

Remember that the body also produces its own fat cells so eating more than you need makes your body store fat. Good fat is essential for energy, gives you that longer-term energy and helps protect your organs.

Healthy foods that are high in fat include:

- Extra virgin olive oil
- Cheese
- Eggs
- Avocados
- Salmon
- Chia seeds
- Nuts
- Full-fat yoghurt

Vitamin and Minerals

Vitamins and minerals are **micronutrients** that support your bodily functions. You only need them in small amounts, but they're still vital to your health and wellbeing.

Vitamins help your body to effectively use other nutrients and to make hormones. There are thirteen essential vitamins and a wide range of minerals that you need to stay fit.

Common signs of vitamin and mineral deficiencies include hair loss and slow healing, but hair loss can also be caused by low estrogen and high levels of testosterone so it's complex. I always like to get your hormones balanced before digging into the detail of what else is going on.

Hair loss is a big worry for perimenopausal women but is still under-researched and not well understood.

FOOD IS BEST

For most adults, food is better than supplements and it's important to follow your doctor's recommendations if you're on a restricted diet. The following foods will make your gut feel loved which in turn will make you feel well.

Fish

Oily fish is excellent as it offers omega-3. This is a fabulous addition to avoid gut inflammation.

The Rainbow

The brightly coloured foods that we have available to us are important for our gut health. Bright fresh produce is telling you clearly that it contains gut-friendly plant nutrients. It will not come in packages but will be as naked as the day it was picked.

One of the most gut-healthy food colours is yellow. Yellow foods are particularly beneficial for your digestion and gut microbiome. They contain antioxidants and help your gut to process and use the food most effectively.

Examples of these are:

- Yellow bell pepper
- Corn
- Onion (I know it's only vaguely yellow!)
- Squash (not quite yellow but still fab!)
- Ginger
- Lemon
- Pineapple

Water

Some experts call water a **macronutrient** because you need a lot of it. Others say it's a **micronutrient** because it doesn't provide energy directly. Some put it in a category all on its own, but I think we all agree it's vital to our wellbeing.

Water from solid foods counts towards your daily intake, so use ingredients like cucumbers, celery, strawberries, cauliflower and cottage cheese.

Even mild dehydration can affect you. If you feel fatigued or have trouble concentrating, you may need to drink more. We should not be waiting until we are thirsty to drink. That is the point when the body is saying *"errr…I'm struggling here"*

SUPERFOODS

Certain foods are known as **superfoods.** These can improve your health by lowering your risk of heart disease and stroke while boosting your energy, focus and mental sharpness.

Here are my favourites:

(Remember to consider intolerances including high histamine foods if it applies to you)

Sweet Potatoes

Sweet potatoes are packed with fibre, potassium and vitamin C. You can cook them in many ways including the usual baked or mashed, but also try cubed in soups.

Blueberries

Blueberries are definitely a superfruit. They contain beneficial antioxidants as well as vitamin C and fibre. They make a healthy treat and they're easy to eat on their own or in smoothies and baked goods like muffins.

Bananas

Bananas make my list because of their high potassium content and healthy dose of vitamin B6.

Broccoli

Broccoli contains a healthy amount of vitamin C and folic acid. If you don't like the taste, you can use some spices, cheese or dip to add flavour.

Spinach

Spinach comes packed with many beneficial ingredients. It is one of the best leafy green vegetables that you can eat. It can be eaten cooked or raw and contains folate, potassium, magnesium, iron and more.

Apples

There's some truth in the saying *'an apple a day keeps the doctor away'*. They contain many of the benefits of the other super-food fruits, as well as having a good fibre content, and they can help you stay full for longer.

Baked Beans

Protein, fibre and calcium are just some of the benefits of this superfood. Some studies show that baked beans are great at helping to protect us because of how they are digested in our gut, so they make a lovely snack or meal to help your gut to help you.

Yogurt

Yogurt is a super healthy way of getting your dairy intake for the day. In addition to being an excellent source of calcium, yogurt has been known to improve overall bowel health by regulating the digestive system.

Salmon

Lean fish are always good alternatives to meat in your diet. However, salmon is extra special because it contains omega 3, which has many health benefits, such as reducing the risk of heart attacks and of psychological problems such as depression.

Olive Oil

Keep in mind that a little goes a long way. Olive oil can lower bad cholesterol levels and it contains a healthy number of antioxidants. Use olive oil mixed with balsamic vinegar for salad dressing instead of the creamy options.

Dark Chocolate

Dark chocolate can be very lovely and is beneficial to your health as it contains those essential antioxidants. It is evidenced to be able to lower blood pressure when eaten in small amounts each day. (Yes I said small amounts!)

Citrus Fruit

The sweet taste of citrus fruits makes them quite a popular superfood. You should aim to eat these fruits in moderation because they have a higher sugar content, but citrus fruits also come with a high amount of vitamin C, fibre and folic acid, which is great.

CHOOSE FRESH

Eating fresh, in-season foods exposes you to new fruits and vegetables; expanding your choice of nutrients, flavours and local, seasonal foods which have more nutrients. Food starts losing nutrients the minute it's picked. With in-season produce, the reduction in time from farm to table keeps the nutrient levels high and foods that travel long distances are often covered in chemicals to help preserve them. In-season foods are also usually less expensive but if these are difficult to obtain then freshly frozen foods are excellent too.

It is more about eating a wide *variety* of fruit and vegetables that our gut really loves. That diversity helps our good bacteria to thrive whilst the bad bacteria die off.

The Seasons

SPRING
Spring is the perfect time to find fresh greens such as spinach, lettuce and broccoli. Leafy green vegetables are a healthy addition to your daily menu and won't add a huge number of calories.

SUMMER
During summer, look for berries such as strawberries which are rich in fibre, collagen (which helps repair gut tissue) and vitamin C (which helps the body to use iron more effectively).

Don't overdo it though as you may end up a bit bloated or dashing to the loo! I clearly remember the time Roger and I experiencing 'apricot overload' after snacking on dried apricots one evening. I don't recommend it.

AUTUMN
Focus on vegetables such as beetroot, carrots, corn, courgettes, potatoes, garlic, and superfruit like cranberries.

WINTER
During winter, you can still find vegetables to keep your nutrition on track. Try kale, broccoli, squash, turnips and potatoes.

It is often a balancing act to ensure you have the right foods to help your overall health. In some cases, your gut has already been upset by years of eating foods that have not necessarily been the most beneficial so it can be a little trial and error to find your own blend of foods that work for you.

PREBIOTICS VERSUS PROBIOTICS

What's the difference?

Very simply, a probiotic is the good bacteria in the gut such as the live bacteria I mentioned earlier in this chapter, and a prebiotic is the food needed for those live bacteria such as fibre.

The whole gut nurturing topic is a vast one and highly individual but in essence, the probiotic is what you need but *not instead* of good nutrition. The prebiotic isn't going to colonise your gut with great bacteria all on its own. That's the job of a probiotic.

Prebiotic foods include:

Garlic, onions, asparagus, chicory, cocoa, ginger, cabbage, fennel, beetroot, bananas, blueberries and apples.

Probiotic foods include:

Kefir, live yoghurt, kombucha, sauerkraut and kimchi.

NUTRITION TIPS

Avoid alcohol and processed sugar. Your gut hates processed sugar and alcohol contains a lot of sugar which will likely irritate and inflame your gut.

Eat slowly. Don't 'inhale' your food. Your gut needs chewed food to be able to deal with it effectively for you.

Cook and smell the food. This helps to get those digestion juices flowing! Takeaways are just not the same.

Try not to eat on the run or at your desk. Being hunched over your laptop or not eating in a relaxed manner can cause bloating and gut transition issues. Believe me… I am an expert at eating on the run or at my desk and my gut never appreciates it.

GUT HEALING AND NUTRIENT VARIETY

It's worth saying again that variety is crucial to a well-rounded diet. Nutritional experts agree that variety is important for gut health because your body needs diversity. Adding a wide variety of fruit and vegetables to each meal is always a good decision.

A good example of this in practice is when dealing with something called small intestinal bacterial overgrowth (SIBO). One of the steps to rid your body of this is to ensure you eat a wide variety of fruit and vegetables every day to feed and encourage your good bacteria whilst starving the bad stuff.

You may also need to mend the lining of your gut which could involve a more complex intervention including introducing foods that help to boost the lining of the gut wall where the vital microbes live. This is often via the FODMAP diet or a scaled down version of it.

There are other foods that help with cleansing that same important gut lining and these include something for both vegetarians and meat eaters such as bone broth, flaxseed, linseeds and oats.

Gut Action

- Start a food intake diary.
- Work on finding ways to increase your water consumption.
- Start to add superfoods to your diet.
- Begin to explore in-season foods and find ways to incorporate them into your diet.

Any nutrition plan must fit in with your life and your budget so use this chapter to help, rather than as a strict guide. Good nutrition alone won't offer you the increased protection during menopause that replacing your missing estrogen can, but they work well together.

If you experience any unusual bloating or pain, please seek advice from a medical professional.

CHAPTER TWELVE

MOVING AND MENOPAUSE

When you're post-menopausal, your natural hormones have mostly left the building so it's important to support your body in different ways.

You don't have the same body as you used to have, but it can still be fit, healthy and working well so let's get you started on the right path to long-term health via a good exercise plan. Clearly, I want you to have your hormones too but whether you decide to take HRT or not, this will help.

In this world of social media and image retouching, the current image of the ideal body is mostly unachievable. It isn't really something to aspire to as it's not real.

I was brought up to think I had to be very slim all the time which just isn't my body shape. When I have been very slim, these were times of huge stress and I looked unwell. You may have been brought up with a totally different understanding of the perfect body, which could be equally damaging, but whatever your experience, we need to treat our bodies differently as we age.

You may know the saying 'Health is Wealth' by Ralph Waldo Emerson. That Ralph Waldo Emerson knew the score even in 1860.

Women's bodies naturally have more fat on them than men's because this is needed for conception, childbearing and menopause.

Men have a much larger amount of testosterone than women, which gives them a leaner body with higher muscle mass and a much higher metabolic rate than women. Women still need testosterone of course, but at a lower level than men.

Expectations of women suggest that they can never be too thin. Being thin is associated with self-control, which is still seen as desirable and admirable, and it's the cultural norm for a woman to struggle with food and body weight.

I remember my lovely mum in hospital, three days before she died, being thrilled when one of the nurses commented on how slim she was. There is something very wrong about that perception of priorities.

That said, being significantly overweight is a health risk and one way to reduce our risk is to exercise regularly. This is not a chapter about losing weight and you may now know that I really dislike diet culture, but a healthy weight is important for everyone, whatever 'a healthy weight 'means to you.

If you don't have regular access to food, the likelihood of a premature death from malnutrition increases. Conversely, if you consume too much food and become overweight, you are more likely to suffer from life impacting diseases.

According to Cancer Research UK, being overweight is the second biggest cause of cancer in the UK, after smoking. That doesn't mean you'll definitely develop cancer, but the more overweight you are and the longer you are overweight, the higher the risk becomes.

When it comes to heart disease, a study carried out by North-western Medicine published in 2018 showed a similar lifespan between optimal weight and overweight people, *but* a higher risk of developing cardiovascular disease at a younger age for those who are overweight.

Adapted from an article by: Alice Dogruyol July 24 2023

Now that we live so much longer than we used to, it isn't uncommon for a third of a woman's life to be her post-meno-pausal years, so starting a regular exercise routine at the peri-menopause stage is a great idea to set us up for a longer and healthier life. Don't panic if you're already post-menopausal, though. It's never too late.

Although you know I'm a huge fan of HRT, it isn't going to solve all your health challenges and you can't expect HRT to remove the need to do some work to help yourself.

That would be great though!

Exercise can really help to reduce menopausal symptoms by strengthening our muscles to support our bones. There are many benefits to taking regular exercise, including:

- Maintaining a healthy weight
- Building muscle mass which helps to protect bones
- Reducing breast cancer risk
- Reducing stress
- Improving mental wellbeing

- Keeping the heart healthy by reducing cholesterol
- Helping prevent type 2 diabetes
- Improving sleep health
- Improving mobility

You should aim to exercise for half an hour a day, five days a week, but a minimum of three times a week. If you can't manage that, then do what you can manage. Some is always better than none.

PLANNING EXERCISE

Planning is key. If it's not in my diary, it doesn't happen! But consider your SMART health goals and only plan realistically otherwise you'll set yourself up not to do it.

Each week, see what you can realistically fit in and commit to it. Find something you like to do. If you don't enjoy it, you won't stick to it so don't join a gym if you hate gyms! It's a waste of your money, time and brain space. You will just feel bad for *not* attending the gym sessions.

Types of Exercise that Work

Resistance Training
This can be as simple as using weights like kettlebells or dumbbells, but yoga and Pilates are also great for muscle mass improvement and strengthening bones.

Cardio
We hear a lot about cardio, and it isn't complicated really. Cardio is anything that will raise your heart rate like running, cycling or even walking. When you raise your heart rate, you

exercise those important vessels and arteries that you can't manage without.

Cold Water

I first tried cold water baths in 2023. They are very invigorating and although there are mixed opinions on actual health benefits, the process is great fun, which is good for the mind too.

Take a look at the Wim Hof Method. You could try a short cold-water session near you at a low cost but do consult the professionals before starting this. I attended a training class before doing an ice bath session, which made it a safe and enjoyable experience.

You may want to extend the water approach to wild water swimming or just swimming in a normal pool if the cold water is too much to take.

Fitness apps are easy and convenient if you have a smartphone or, try a few free YouTube videos of any fitness routine you fancy.

You may like to start going to classes, join a walking group or maybe sign up to a course with a personal trainer.

It is important to start slowly if you haven't exercised in a while. Have a chat with your doctor before getting started if it's all a bit new to you.

NATURAL OR OPPORTUNISTIC MOVEMENT

What do we mean by natural movement?

This is all about taking advantage of opportunities throughout the day without making a big fuss over it. I love the simplicity of this approach and you may find me dancing to my favourite sounds whilst brushing my teeth - I couldn't possibly confirm that.

It is not a big event. It is just about adding movement to your everyday activities that doesn't seem like exercise; by looking at how you can do your daily tasks in a way that makes you more active.

When you become an **opportunistic exerciser,** you increase your chances of staying with it for the long haul.

As I've said already, it's important to bear in mind that something is better than nothing. Viewing activity in this way helps you to get out of the all-or-nothing mindset which diminishes your chances of sticking with an exercise routine. Even small amounts of physical activity can provide positive health benefits. While regular exercise is the best way to receive the health benefits of physical activity, it can often be a challenge to make time for a lengthy workout.

Start by thinking about where you are every day: work, home or with friends and family and how you can add a little something to each place and activity.

TOO CONVENIENT

What this comes down to is making things a little less convenient for yourself.

Everything these days has been upgraded with easy-to-use machines or appliances, making life easier in many ways, but there is also a downside. Technology reduces our opportunities to be physically active throughout the day.

The more we move, the more muscles we use and the more calories we burn. Those effects add up.

Here are some examples:

- Have walking meetings instead of sitting down
- Plant and tend a garden
- Wash your car yourself instead of using the car wash
- Clean your driveway
- Do squats or have a dance whilst you brush your teeth
- Carry shopping instead of using a trolly, whenever possible
- Do calf raises whilst you talk on the phone
- Do planks, sit-ups or stretches whilst watching TV

What two or three ways could you add natural movement into your day right now?

Tackle that Mindset

Learn to love the feeling of being active, the feeling of moving your body, stretching your muscles, and feeling your heart beat faster. It is definitely a sensation you can come to look forward to, but **it starts with your mindset.**

If you notice yourself saying things like, *"Ugh. I hate exercise,"* try stopping yourself from having this narrative because your brain hears you. I cover more on this in the mindset chapter.

What you tell yourself is what your mind believes. If you challenge those stories you're telling yourself, you can begin to see they're not the truth.

Movement Action

What is your current belief about exercise? If this is a negative thought, what's the exact opposite? What if you were someone who loved to exercise? What would that be like?

Do you start exercise plans with the best intentions of getting in shape, but have trouble staying with anything long enough to see the benefits? Developing a personal exercise plan that you can stick to will help you lead a longer and healthier life.

CREATING A PERSONAL EXERCISE PLAN

Clarify your goals. Moderate exercise may be all you need if you want to improve your overall health and feel more energetic. If you have your heart set on running a marathon, though, you'll need more targeted preparations!

What are your exercise goals? Remember to take a balanced approach.

A comprehensive exercise plan includes three key components:

- Strength
- Flexibility
- Cardiovascular fitness

If you want to save time, there are many ways to combine your training. For example, swimming will strengthen your heart and muscles at the same time.

Schedule It

The number one reason people claim they don't exercise regularly is a lack of time.

You make time for a variety of other things every day: taking a shower, driving to and from work and watching television; so, make an appointment with yourself to get the exercise your body needs to be as healthy as it possibly can.

Create a simple exercise schedule

When is the best time for you to exercise each day/week?

Try to enlist support or find a workout buddy

The number two reason people don't exercise is boredom or loneliness.

Get out there with a good friend, your significant other or just on your own to start with but in a place where you will meet people. It is good to spend time with others and can make things a lot more enjoyable. A workout partner will also make you feel a greater sense of responsibility. No-one likes to let other people down.

Getting fit can be fun if you add in a social component. Who could you ask to join you as an exercise buddy?

Vary Your Workouts

Avoid boredom by mixing up your activities. Visit a new yoga studio or do your tai chi outdoors when the weather is pleasant. Come up with a variety of activities. There's no reason you can't swim one day, walk the next, and play ball sports the day after that.

Generate a list of a few different exercise options that you might enjoy. Think about everything on offer and keep yourself entertained as well.

Make It Easy

I don't mean you should make the exercise easy. Sorry about that. I mean make it easy to get to the point of starting the exercise. Driving halfway across town in rush hour traffic is enough for anyone to find an excuse to skip a day.

The truth is that the gym isn't necessary. A simple set of weights, a skipping rope, or some running shoes are probably all you really need. You may even have a basketball court or a tennis court at your local park.

Anticipate Obstacles

Identify potential interruptions and make contingency plans. You could buy a second-hand treadmill to have on hand for those days when bad weather keeps you indoors or take a skipping rope with you when you travel. Weighted hula hoops are a great option as well as being inexpensive. Great exercise for your core.

Track Your Progress

It is a lot easier to stay interested and motivated when you can see some real progress.

Fortunately, progress comes quickly at the beginning of any exercise programme so devise a test of your fitness that you can do occasionally. It can be simple, like how many push-ups you can do or how long it takes you to walk a mile.

Reward Yourself

Celebrate your progress with rewards. Treat yourself to a new set of dumbbells or book a massage when you achieve a goal.

Design

Design your format. If you're technology savvy, organise your data with a mobile app on your phone.

If you prefer pen and paper, buy a notebook with a motivational cover. You know I love pen and paper.

Define Your Scope

You may want to track just the basics or paint a more detailed picture. As a minimum, try to capture how long your workout lasted and the level of intensity.

YOUR CYCLE CAN HELP

Many women find it helpful to understand how their emotions and hormones affect their fitness plans.

If you are still having periods, there are days in your cycle that will be better for your exercise routine. Of course, your cycle will likely not be the textbook twenty-eight days long so try to chart your individual cycle to plan more effectively.

Days 1-7
Hormone levels are lowest at the start of the cycle when you have your period, and energy levels can be low.

This may make you feel that you don't want to exercise, but exercise reduces the hormone responsible for inflammation and cramps, so it is worth exercising even if you don't want to. Your best options will be things like swimming, yoga, walking and cycling.

Days 7-13
When your period ends, your estrogen is higher, and you may feel more energetic, so consider strength training or high-intensity exercise.

Be careful as your ligaments are more relaxed from now, which may increase your chance of injury.

Day 14
This is the perfect time to build your muscles during your workout routine so aim to do high-intensity workouts, such as circuit training and running.

Days 20-23
Time to take things easier on yourself. Progesterone is high and can make you tired and more likely to overheat. Aim for aerobic exercises such as swimming, dancing or Pilates.

Days 24-28
Long walks and yoga are a great option here and aim to eat slow-release carbs, such as oats, beans and pulses, wholegrain rice and quinoa.

Updates

Recording your performance on the spot helps to ensure accuracy. Experiment with a system that will work for you. That could mean bringing your notebook to the gym, filling it out before bed or there are plenty of apps on which to track your progress.

Vary Your Routine

Your body adapts to any familiar movement, so walking a mile will soon require less effort than it used to. If you want to advance, you'll need to make things more challenging.

Many experts suggest that a ten percent weekly increase in weight, intensity or distance is usually a safe guide.

Review Your Records

Reflect on how far you've come. Maybe you've worked your way up from five push-ups to fifteen over the course of the year.

Speak with Others

Reserve your notes for your eyes alone if you prefer, or you can share them with others. Your doctor or personal trainer can give you more detailed recommendations when they learn more about you.

Movement Action

- Begin finding ways in your day to add natural movement.
- Create a positive narrative about exercise.
- Create your personal exercise plan.
- Choose a method for keeping track of your progress and begin using it.

Chapter Thirteen

MINDSET AND MENOPAUSE

A positive mindset is key to success when managing our health and wellness.

Your mind is on your side although it may seem otherwise when you're waking up with palpitations and anxiety. When you give it the right feedback and encouragement, you can help it to help you.

If you continually tell yourself you're unattractive, your mind will believe that as fact and your self-esteem and confidence will be shot to pieces.

When I worked as a body positivity coach, I would encourage clients to say something positive about themselves **out loud** when they looked in the mirror. It works, I promise. Eventually, your brain believes what you tell it, and this becomes your new normal.

If you've ever done any cognitive behavioural therapy, you'll know this approach.

WRITING

If you've got this far, you'll know I'm a huge fan of writing things down to focus the mind. Seeing things on paper is a little different from just thinking about them. Reviewing your thoughts can be a powerful tool for change and growth. However, given my small obsession with stationery perhaps I would say that.

Your notes will provide the insight for you to make positive changes. If the concept of menopause and HRT is new to you, try to make note-taking a regular habit. Write in your new sexy little notebook weekly or even daily, and it will become second nature. I find writing quite calming, but more importantly, it ensures I remain focused on my goals which is always a challenge for me.

Your notes will help you track how you feel and your subsequent improvements.

Review Your Day

If you're making your notes in the evening, begin each entry by reviewing your day.

What Happened?

Record anything you might want to remember in the future, whether it's a day or years in the future. Be willing to be honest with yourself. It is useful to have this written memory when trying to join the dots of any challenges and it will aid future conversations with therapists, doctors or other specialists.

Having to dig around in your mind for your symptoms and HRT history when asked to do so by specialists, is quite stressful. I love it when a client arrives with a list detailing her health history!

Write about any challenges you're facing with menopause, HRT and in your life but also write about the successes, and remember: Not everything is HRT or menopause related. You may improve with changes to your lifestyle or nutrition. You are a complex being but doing your best to feel healthy doesn't need to be complex.

GOALS

Most of us have a vague idea of what we'd like to accomplish, but we don't all have true, concrete goals.

Without a goal, you drift along hoping for things to improve.

With a goal, you have a definite direction and purpose.

Though we've all been told how important targets are, few of us have ever been given specific directions regarding how to formulate an effective goal.

Many years ago, when I was working in senior training and management roles, these goal-setting approaches were part of my training sessions. They haven't changed much, because they work, so you may know about them already, although these days I adapt them to my wellness world.

They are important steps to achieving the level of health and positive action you want and deserve.

SMART Health Goals

SMART goals are not new news, but you can adapt the process to suit your health, resulting in SMART Health Goals.

S - Specific
Be as specific as you need to be, but don't get too het up with the detail, such as needing to know estrogen blood level results before starting HRT. It is important to have a clear target but being too specific limits your success.

For example: HRT isn't a health bullet. It is great and it works, but it takes time, perseverance and the correct information to assess what you need.

Whatever you plan to do, just start it.

M – Measurable
If you can't measure it, how will you know if you've achieved it? How will you know if you're making progress?

Goals that deal with your symptoms or body weight are easy to quantify. A goal to take a trip is also easy to measure because you either did it or you didn't.

Goals that deal with less quantifiable characteristics, such as whether you feel better than you did, can be a little more challenging. You might be best to develop your own measuring scale. I often suggest to clients that we look at the last time they felt well and work from there to discover what has changed since then.

Ensure your goal can be measured before you get started.

A – Achievable

Start with a goal that's achievable enough for you to believe it can be done within the timeframe you've set. Do you have the necessary resources, support and time to achieve what you want to achieve?

If you need support to give up smoking, make sure you allow time to access that. Do not set yourself up for failure with an unreachable goal such as losing 28 lbs in four weeks or giving up smoking within a week when you have been on 40 cigarettes a day for 20 years or more.

R – Relevant

Your actions need to be relevant to your long-term goal. That may seem obvious but it's easy to become sidelined with non-relevant or unhelpful actions.

If you're trying to improve your sleep, your actions probably initially need to focus on changing your pre-sleep routine and sleep hygiene rather than deciding what to eat for breakfast.

You may feel more comfortable scrolling social media and asking for help online about a health problem, but you actually need to make an appointment with your doctor.

We've all done that, but again, your action needs to match your long-term goal which is to remove the anxiety and improve your wellness.

T - Time-bound

Without a timeline, you might find yourself waiting a long

time because you're unlikely to ever get started! Believe me, I have a gold medal in procrastination.

Having an end date creates focus. I gave myself an end date to finish writing this book for that very reason. My publisher will fine me a lot of money if I am late with my manuscript! That's enough motivation for me and I know I need to be held accountable.

An effective end date for most tasks is usually no more than twelve weeks into the future. Anything beyond twelve weeks can cause your focus to wane. It is too easy to procrastinate with goals set too far in the future. If your goal will take longer than that, break it into smaller goals.

Mindset Action

- Start making notes: Specifically start noting your cycle (if you still have one) and your symptoms, depending on where you are in your HRT and menopause pathway.
- Set your personal SMART Health Goals

Things only change when new actions are taking place. If nothing changes, nothing changes.

Chapter Fourteen

MENOPAUSAL NOT MAD

In Chapter Four I left you pondering the benefits of the hormone therapy which really helped me after the birth of my second child in the 1990s. I knew at that stage that my body had done enough and if you've read Chapter Seven on hysterectomy and prolapse, you'll understand, so I chose to have a sterilisation.

I received some quite judgmental criticism from other mums for my choice to be sterilised in my early thirties which was fairly unhelpful. It was the right decision for me, and I have never regretted not giving birth to more children. I think my pelvic floor is grateful too.

When my youngest was around two years old, I split from my first husband with every intention of being a single parent, but three months later I met Roger and within three days I knew he was the one.

Now, after twenty-three years, we have experienced a lot of life's challenges together and we're a great team. I think I'll keep him.

Since we met in 2001 and subsequently married in 2008, Roger has had the unique pleasure of accompanying me on my path to becoming peri then post-menopausal. I expect he's super grateful for that but best not ask him just in case.

I didn't want to make this chapter a big old moan fest about my symptoms, as I stand by my comment that it's an absolute privilege to be here to experience it, but it definitely wasn't easy. I have huge empathy with all peri and post-menopausal women who fight to be heard.

I now know I was about thirty-seven when I became peri-menopausal but with a fairly new relationship, a family to care for and the usual stresses of life, the early symptoms were masked. My list of symptoms was slowly increasing, even if they seemed unconnected.

My main challenges (other than my prolapsed bowel as outlined in the hysterectomy chapter) were my erratic mood, an extreme buzzing in my head and an overall feeling of being unhappy. I would often refer to this as a lack of joy for life. I was erratically itchy, anxious, sweaty and like many of the women I speak with, I felt as if I was just not myself anymore.

A while ago I counted the number of symptoms I had at the peak of perimenopause and my number was at least twen-ty-nine of the forty-plus symptoms on offer. I decided to research HRT as I knew my mum had been very happy with hers and that this was a route I wanted to take.

Little did I know that this topic was so contentious and that it was about to become a huge part of my life, both personally and professionally. However, I didn't wake up one morning, decide to take HRT and everything returned to normal the next day. With the best will in the world, that's not how it works.

It was a process of elimination and perhaps like you, I was pushed from pillar to post by doctors who just had no understanding of perimenopause. Many considered HRT to be a very negative option if an option at all.

The result of this was that I was prescribed anti-depressants which I didn't take, and I was sent for counselling which I thoroughly enjoyed as I got on very well with the counsellor. She agreed that I didn't need her services. Later I was prescribed the wrong HRT regime for my needs and given the impression that I was a needy time waster.

When I was told that HRT wasn't a good idea as I would '*definitely get breast cancer*', I knew I needed to take control of, and responsibility for, my own hormone health. Although Menopausal Not Mad® was not founded until 2018, I was working hard to learn about menopause and HRT long before then.

Having said all that, there were some fabulous medics who were happy to be led by me and my desires for my future health so, I was finally able to start getting my hormones on track. I have tried most HRT regimes in my time as I like to live my message that patience and perseverance is key to success.

It takes time to know what works for you but there are some basic starting points for everyone. I know you want me to list all the HRT regime options here, but it really is very individual and ploughing through a list of them is not safe or helpful as you need a proper assessment based on you and your history.

I can, however, share my own HRT pathway to demonstrate the need for an open mind and flexibility.

In order, I have tried:

- Sequential combined tablets
- Sequential combined patches
- Oestrogel and sequential Utrogestan
- Oestrogel and continuous Utrogestan
- Sandrena gel and continuous Utrogestan
- Oestrogel and double continuous Utrogestan
- Oestrogel, double Utrogestan and the mini pill (to stop post-menopausal bleeding)
- Estrogen patches and continuous Utrogestan
- Estrogen patches and double continuous Utrogestan
- Estrogen-only patches (post-hysterectomy)

I also added in testosterone a few years ago which notably has helped my bones to feel stronger and less painful and I can confirm that as yet I haven't grown a beard or a penis!

In 2017 I was pondering my working life and looking at a change. I felt that my passion for women's health and menopause, specifically HRT, was organically developing into a movement that needed to be nurtured and in 2018, *Menopausal Not Mad®* was born.

I started small, offering support to friends. Then, with permission from the admin of some Facebook groups, I started to offer evidence-based guidance on a wider scale, where HRT was and still is in some cases, mostly vilified.

It was tough at times and online abuse became a regular thing in my life. Sadly, it has become quite usual in this keyboard driven world and there is still a lot of negativity around the topic of HRT, but it has never dampened my passion for my role.

In 2020 I opened my own online group focusing on HRT facts and support, which, over a period of just under four years, has grown to a membership of nearly 40,000 across more than one hundred countries. My priority was always to offer only fact-based HRT guidance and we quickly gained a reputation for exactly that.

In 2022, about a week after my hysterectomy and bowel prolapse repair, I was proud to receive international acknowledgment from META (Facebook) for my community support, which included six months of free support and guidance working with the META team and all that this brought with it.

2024 has since been a year of change for *Menopausal Not Mad*.

We have grown and developed as a direct result of community needs and requests but also as a result of my own development within the female wellness space. I have continued with my learning which has included the study of trauma-informed coaching, sleep counselling and further nutrition study all alongside ongoing HRT research of course.

In 2024 I made the decision to pass the baton of my online HRT group to someone with the same passion and love for the role as me. Whilst I am still involved with the group, the members benefit from a fresh perspective at the helm. I am so happy to know it is in good hands.

Chapter Fifteen

REAL PEOPLE

I have so many reports of peri and post-menopausal fear, confusion and dismissal of female health challenges but most are anonymous.

I recently asked for updated comments from anyone in my community who felt they wanted to openly share their menopause and HRT experience.

I have been overwhelmed with the number of responses and have selected just a few to demonstrate that you're not alone.

'Putting up with' symptoms and health challenges is just not necessary, and your hormones are there to help you thrive.

There are exceptions to everything and it's always your choice but now you know you *have* choices.

QUOTES FROM MY MENOPAUSE COMMUNITY

If I didn't use your quote and you're reading this, please know that I could have filled at least two books with quotes alone, so I had to make some choices. I am grateful you took the time to respond. I will treasure your words and will likely use them in other areas of my work.

Thank you for trusting me with your menopause challenges.

I have detailed the following examples with full permission from the particular people to whom they refer.

"The worst thing was the vaginal dryness. It started when I was about forty years old, and I didn't know what it was. I suffered with thrush nearly every month and needed to pee more often. I was frightened about the cancer risks with HRT, but it has changed my life."

— **Sally Godwin**

"I went from a suicidal shell of a woman to the me I recognised again after only a couple of weeks on HRT."

— **Claire Mills**

"HRT was a life changer! Overnight the anxiety and awful cold sweats vanished. I felt back to the normal me."

— **Lynsey Spedding**

"You can't fix a hormone deficiency with lifestyle changes alone."

— Jennifer Bourke

"I woke up one day and wanted to hide from the world. I felt like I had disappeared. HRT saved me from constant anxiety and daily migraines."

— Jayne Hill

"My husband is a lovely supportive man. We have been married thirty-three years and we are approaching sixty. He says there is no way I can live without my HRT!"

— Jane Dippolito

"HRT is not one size fits all and finding Menopausal Not Mad made me realise just how many women are suffering symptoms and that I'm not alone."

— Susan Baron

"I'd lost myself totally and then thankfully I found HRT."

— Sue Patterson

"I started my HRT journey in 2021 and had only heard scare-mongering stories about it. I stumbled upon Jane, and her no-nonsense approach to offering information and advice has been invaluable in navigating and understanding the minefield of HRT."

— **Ella Cutler**

"At sixty-nine years, HRT has helped to have strong bones and a healthy heart. It has enabled me to run and strength train, so I am physically and mentally strong enough to compete in fitness competitions with athletes thirty or forty years younger than me."

— **Anne O'Donoghue**

"I realised that my hormones were seriously out of whack a year after my second failed IVF treatment and was desperate to gain some level of normality. My consultant was happy to prescribe HRT which I take successfully to this day."

— **Ange King**

"I had suffered with vertigo for five years. I started HRT and it had completely gone within five days."

— **Denise Bassett**

"HRT has drastically helped my mental health. The depression and anxiety I had never felt before having now been relieved."

— Jasmine Reed

"Starting HRT was honestly like finding a glorious sunny day after so much darkness."

— Tiffany Swayne

"In 2020 I was bruised and battered from my GP refusing to accept that my numerous symptoms were menopause related. I was told I had depression, simply because I had not had a hot sweat. I loved Jane's professional, up-to-date, no-nonsense, evidence-based advice from the start. There was nowhere else as well-informed and supportive. I now check in with Jane once a year and feel very much that she is my menopause guardian angel. With her help and encouragement, I can advocate for myself in a system that is at best naive and at worst negligent."

— Karen Smith

CONCLUSION

The topic of menopause and my valued *Menopausal Not Mad* community are precious to me and I'd love to tell you that when you take HRT, your hormones will be totally perfect and life's going to be a dream, with your HRT all balanced, and you eating only fresh organic foods made in a kitchen filled with rainbows and dreams, but that probably isn't going to happen.

HRT needs tweaking and adjusting over time and an expectation of one hundred percent perfection with hormone balance is not realistic, but we can all do more to help those tricky little hormones to help us.

Menopause and ageing can be challenging, and any changes to your circumstances will make a difference just as they did when you were young and not even thinking about menopause. The changes require patience, an open mind and consistency to be effective, but being hormonally balanced has been my starting point since I began to understand what my body needed.

My HRT is my saviour, but I treat it with respect and never take it for granted. Any stress, illness or significant life change can knock me off balance, but just knowing that makes it so much easier to manage.

HRT is not the **only** factor in my wellbeing, but it is the reason I can function with almost no menopausal symptoms. I still have some tinnitus but I just zone that out and I feel positive and reassured that I am helping my body to fend off osteoporosis, heart disease and other nasties.

In addition, I have made a lot of nutritional changes including healing my poor unhappy gut, dealing with a wheat intolerance and of course, evicting an ovarian cancer.

For now, I will continue to fight for every woman to have the choice to take the hormones they need without judgment or accusations of being addicted to their natural hormones or of being swept up in a sea of mass hysteria.

That learning continues onward and I have lots of plans to do more.

More books.

More support.

Just more.

Menopause has not stopped me, and it shouldn't stop you.

MY SUMMARY TIPS

Expecting perfection with your health is not realistic but you can expect more than you are told you should.

- Share but don't compare. You are unique.
- Persistence is paramount. Any changes to HRT, nutrition or lifestyle can take time to settle.
- Worry won't help your hormones so try to find something to help you to relax. This will be different for everyone but for me, just a bit of greenery on a walk can restore my mindset to a calm and open-minded place.
- I am very productive when I'm away from technology which brings me back to my lovely notebook obsession.

Now I must dash... I have an appointment with my stationery specialist.

Wishing you happy hormones, you lovely human.

Jane x

P.S - If you want to know how you can work with me to get yourself back on track, you can find me on:

My website:
https://www.menopausalnotmad.co.uk

My Instagram:
https://www.instagram.com/menopausalnotmad/

My Facebook page:
https://www.facebook.com/menopausalnotmad/

You can also *email me* on:
jane@menopausalnotmad.co.uk

BIBLIOGRAPHY

www.mind.org

Bluming Dr A and Tavris C (2018) *Oestrogen Matters*

www.menopausalnotmad.co.uk

https://www.menopausalnotmad.co.uk/wp-content/
uploads/2024/04/2024-The-Misdiagnosis-Mistreatment-
of-Women-19th-Century-Today.pdf

www.themenopausecharity.org

National Institute for Health and Care Excellence (NICE):
*Guidance on professional standards and ethics for doctors
Decision making and consent* 9th November 2020
https://www.menopausalnotmad.co.uk/wp-content/
uploads/2021/02/updated-decision-making-and-
consent-guidance_pdf-84160128.pdf

https://www.whi.org/

British Menopause Society (BMS) Guidelines: *The
management of unscheduled bleeding on hormone
replacement therapy (HRT)*: April 2024 update
https://thebms.org.uk/publications/bms-joint-
guidelines/management-of-unscheduled-bleeding-on-
hormone-replacement-therapy-hrt/

National Public Radio (NPR):
https://www.npr.org/sections/health-
shots/2024/05/01/1248525256/hormones-menopause-
hormone-therapy-hot-flashes

Harper Collins Publishers 2024
https://www.collinsdictionary.com/dictionary/english/
journalling

https://www.histamineintolerance.org.uk/about/the-food-
diary/the-food-list/

https://www.fda.gov/news-events/press-announcements/
fda-approves-first-oral-treatment-postpartum-
depression

Women's Health Concern
https://thebms.org.uk/wp-content/uploads/2022/12/15-
BMS-TfC-HRT-preparations-and-equivalent-
alternatives-NOV2022-A.pdf